OFFAL

GOURMET COOKERY FROM HEAD TO TAIL

Jana Allen and Margaret Gin

Pitman Publishing

First published in the United States 1974
First published in Great Britain 1976

Pitman Limited
Pitman House, 39 Parker Street, London WC2B 5PB

Sir Isaac Pitman and Sons Limited
Banda Street, P.O. Box 46038, Nairobi, Kenya

Pitman Publishing Co. S.A. (Pty) Limited
Craighall Mews, Jan Smuts Avenue, Craighall Park, Johannesburg 2001, South Africa

This edition has been adapted for British readers by Helena Radecka
from the original publication by 101 Publications, San Francisco.

ISBN: 0 273 00958 3

Text set in 11/13 pt IBM Press Roman, printed by photolithography,
and bound in Great Britain at The Pitman Press, Bath.

(117:17)

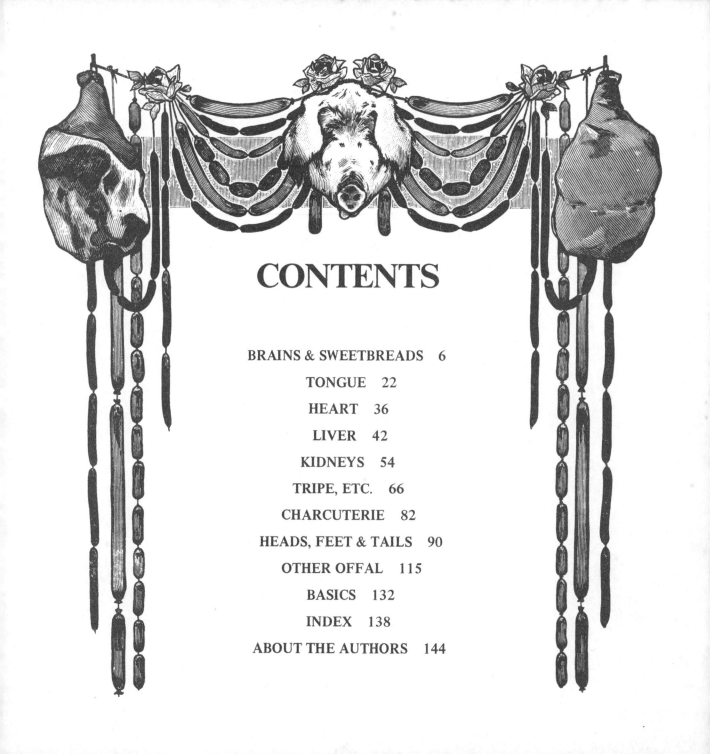

CONTENTS

PREFACE

Throughout recorded history innards and other variety meats have been an important part of man's diet. They have been present on tables of both kings and peasants, worth a king's ransom at one time, eaten for survival in another. Offal — tongue, heart, brains, liver, feet, tails, etc. — includes some of the most flavorful of all meats which are considered to be among the greatest delicacies of culinary art.

The ancient Chinese gathered thousands of duck tongues for a single meal and the tongues of larks were a favorite of the Elizabethans. For centuries the Scots have made their haggis from the innards of sheep mixed with onions, suet and oatmeal. Tripes à la mode de Caen and countless variations of sweetbreads are classics of provincial French cuisine. Pioneers crossing the North American continent spread their bread with the rich, buttery marrow of buffalo and served up the entrails in a hearty "son-of-a-bitch" stew.

However, in recent times, innards have often been neglected. In a world that has been spoiled by an excess of "beef and butter", they have come to be viewed as symbols of poverty. Abundance has been taken for granted and, with it, there has been an appalling waste and abuse of natural resources. We are just beginning to grasp the consequences. And, clearly, it is time for ingenuity.

That's where innards come in. They are recognized as a staple in our quest for survival. Not only are they becoming more available but they are also, for the most part, reasonably priced and highly nutritious, and their uses are boundless. Once the basic cooking techniques are mastered, only the imagination limits the vast range of delicious dishes that can be created.

Quite simply, innards are begging to be understood. It is for this reason we present this book.

Jana Allen
Margaret Gin

BRAINS & SWEETBREADS

For many centuries, brains and sweetbreads have been found on the dinner table — whether esteemed as a great delicacy or eaten merely for nourishment in times of scarcity. Men of ancient times devoured the thymus (sweetbreads) of their freshly killed beasts and boiled or roasted the heads, extracting the brains, which were considered one of the best morsels of all. An edict of the state in ancient Greece, in about the fifth century, B.C., proscribed eating brains on the grounds that it was like eating the heads of one's parents, during the days of the Roman Empire, brains were used in almost every forcemeat, a preparation which survives to this day. And, although dietary laws of the day forbade serving many variety meats at banquets, enthusiastic epicures were not curtailed for long. At the height of the Italian Renaissance, when hedonistic pleasures and extravagance reigned, such dishes as pheasant and peacock brains were highly prized and enjoyed.

According to Platina, the renowned gourmet of 15th century Italy, overindulgence in brains could bring about phlegmatic humor. He also noted that brains should always be consumed at the beginning of dinner, else risk the chance of upsetting the stomach. His book includes a recipe for the common preparation of calf brains (pickled in vinegar, mint and herbs), a dish that it was believed would increase fertility and loosen bowels if consumed by those of a warm nature. Common beliefs of the medicinal properties of brains also included the use of hare and rabbit brains as antidotes for poisons and the idea that the brains of birds were more nutritious than those of beasts.

Brains and sweetbreads rose to the pinnacle of their popularity during the 19th century when the chefs of *haute cuisine* sauced them *à la Perigourdine, à la Financière, à la Nantua* or *au beurre* (or *beurre noir* for brains). Then they could be found on every banquet menu of note. In the 20th century, brains and sweetbreads continue to be enjoyed. They may be scrambled for breakfast, added to forcemeats (as in the Italian *zampone*), braised in stock (Chinese brain soup) or steamed within the breast cavity of fowl. But we feel there is one serious misconception regarding brains and sweetbreads. Although they may be used interchangeably in most recipes, each has a flavor and texture distinctively different from the other. Most people who like brains will enjoy sweetbreads, but the reverse is not always true.

PREPARATION OF BRAINS

As with all soft organ meats, brains should be bought and prepared when absolutely fresh. They are very perishable and should always be eaten within 24 hours of purchasing. Fresh brains look very shiny and pinkish grey in color. The outside membrane should be moist, giving a plump, unshriveled appearance. If the brains are fresh, the outer membrane will slip easily from the meat; if they are not, the membrane has a tendency to stick to the crevices.

Step I: Soaking and Cleaning
Soak brains in cold water to cover for 30 minutes. (This step should never be eliminated.) Rinse under cold running water and drain. Remove arteries and outer membranes with a pointed knife. (Some cooks prefer to remove membranes after parboiling. Furthermore, it is not absolutely essential to remove the membrane; some cooks eliminate this step entirely.) Brains should be free of any trace of blood.

Step II: Parboiling
Parboil brains by placing them in a saucepan with cold water to cover, adding 2 tablespoons vinegar or lemon juice for each 1-1/2 pints of water. Bring to a gentle boil, reduce heat and simmer for 5 to 15 minutes, depending on the size and variety of brains selected. Veal and lamb brains require a shorter cooking period than beef brains. Do not allow water to come to a full rolling boil. (Parboiling in acidulated water helps retain shape and whiteness.) Other ingredients may be added to the cooking liquid for flavor enrichment, if desired.

When parboiling is completed, either plunge the brains into cold water or allow them to cool in the cooking liquid. These treatments help firm up the meat, making it hold its shape when used whole or sliced for recipes. Drain well and chill brains in a covered glass jar or bowl until ready to use.

BRAIN CAVIAR

3/4 pound calf brains
white wine vinegar
3 tablespoons salad oil
1 or more cloves garlic, finely chopped
3 tablespoons lemon juice
1 teaspoon grated lemon peel
2 tablespoons finely chopped chives
2 tablespoons finely chopped
   black olives
salt and white pepper to taste
3 tablespoons chopped parsley

Soak, clean and parboil brains according to Steps I and II in basic instructions, using white wine vinegar in parboiling liquid. Immediately plunge brains into cold water; pat dry with paper towels. Press cooled brains through a sieve. Slowly combine oil with brains, stirring all the while, until mixture is smooth. Then add garlic, lemon juice and peel, chives, black olives, salt and pepper. Mound in a dish and garnish with parsley. Serve with unsalted melba toast.
Serves 4 as an appetizer.

BRAIN VINAIGRETTE

To make a brain vinaigrette, prepare brains as for brain caviar, omitting the olives and substituting 1 teaspoon prepared mustard, 1 teaspoon sugar and 2 teaspoons each chopped onion and chopped sweet pickle. The vinaigrette may be thinned out with a little vinegar and oil, if desired. This cold sauce is nice on salad greens as well as on cold pickled pigs' feet or tongue.

BRAIN PÂTÉ

3/4 pound calf brains
8 tablespoons scalded milk
8 tablespoons bread crumbs
4 eggs
1 clove garlic
3 tablespoons chopped spring onions
dash of nutmeg
4 tablespoons butter
1/2 teaspoon salt
1/4 teaspoon white pepper
chopped parsley for garnish

Soak and clean brains according to Step I in basic instructions. Combine scalded milk and bread crumbs and blend well; let cool. Purée cleaned brains and eggs in a blender; add bread-crumb mixture and remaining ingredients. Pour into a well-buttered 1-1/2-pint baking dish or tin. Place in a larger pan with 1 inch of boiling water. Bake in a 300°F oven for 45 minutes, or until set (when sides begin to shrink). Leave in pan 5 minutes before turning out on serving platter. Garnish with chopped parsley.
Serves 4

Variation: Allow baked pâté to cool slightly; then chill in refrigerator. To make aspic coating combine 1 cup clear beef stock with 2 tablespoons dry sherry or Madeira and 2 teaspoons unflavored gelatine. Heat gently until quite clear. Paint entire surface of chilled pâté 4 to 5 times, chilling after each application. Garnish with chopped parsley. Serve as an hors d'oeuvre or as a first course, sliced, and arranged on lettuce leaves, along with gherkins, Dijon-style mustard and crusty French bread.

CREAMY CHOWDER

1/2 pound calf brains
2 large carrots, diced
1 large potato, diced
2 stalks celery, diced
4 tablespoons butter
1 onion, finely chopped
3 tablespoons flour
salt and freshly ground pepper
5 ounces fresh peas or corn kernels
 (optional)
2 egg yolks, beaten
2 tablespoons chopped parsley

Bring carrots, potatoes and celery to a boil with 3 pints water; reduce heat and simmer for 30 minutes. Prepare brains according to Steps I and II in basic instructions, parboiling for 5 minutes only; dice. Then heat butter in a frying pan; sauté brains with onion. Stir in flour, salt and pepper. Then add brain mixture and peas to vegetable pot, stirring all ingredients well; continue cooking 10 minutes longer. Add 1/2 cup of the vegetable stock to egg yolks, stirring constantly to prevent eggs from curdling. Just before serving, gradually add egg yolks to soup, stirring constantly. Stir in parsley and serve with crusty bread.
Serves 6 to 8

BRAIN QUENELLES

1/2 pound calf brains
8 tablespoons or more bread crumbs
8 tablespoons hot milk
4 tablespoons butter, softened
2 eggs
1 tablespoon sherry
1/2 teaspoon salt
dash of white pepper
dash of nutmeg

Good, hard French bread crumbs are essential to this recipe, both for flavor and texture. Thoroughly dry out bread on the kitchen counter or in the oven; then pulverize in the blender. They must be made at home; supermarket "cottonwool" bread cannot be substituted.
Soak, clean and parboil brains according to Steps I and II in basic instructions. Drain well and pat dry. Combine hot milk and bread crumbs together to form a smooth paste; let cool. Finely chop brains and combine with butter and bread-crumb paste until well blended. Add eggs one at a time, mixing well after each addition. Add sherry, salt, pepper and nutmeg. Adjust seasoning.

To form quenelles, roll out a scant tablespoon of the mixture, one at a time, onto a floured board and shape into sausages, about 3 inches long by 1/2 inch thick. Repeat until mixture is used up. Line quenelles in a buttered pan. Add boiling water just to cover; poach in simmering water for 10 minutes, making sure water does not boil again. Remove quenelles with slotted spoon. Place on a heated platter and serve with a curried Béchamel sauce (page 133).
Makes 36 quenelles; serves 6 to 8 as a first course or light luncheon dish.

Variation: Sweetbreads may be substituted for brains.

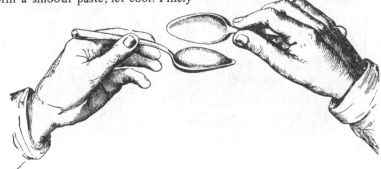

9

FRIED BRAINS

1-1/2 pounds calf or lamb brains
1 small onion
1/4 teaspoon salt
4 tablespoons lemon juice
2 tablespoons olive oil
2 tablespoons finely chopped parsley
flour seasoned with salt and pepper
2 eggs, beaten
vegetable oil for deep-frying

Soak, clean and parboil brains according to Steps I and II of basic instructions, using vinegar and adding an onion and salt to parboiling liquid. Plunge into cold water. Cut cooled brains into pieces; put in a bowl with lemon juice, olive oil and parsley. Let marinate 1 hour. Drain pieces of brain and pat dry. Roll in flour, then dip into beaten egg. Deep-fry until a pale golden color in hot oil. Drain on paper towels and serve immediately with lemon wedges, tartare sauce, lemon-flavored ketchup or ketchup spiced with a dash of Tabasco and cinnamon. Serves 6

BRAIN & SPINACH CAKES

1 pound brains (any kind)
1 pound fresh spinach, blanched, well drained and chopped, or 12 ounces chopped frozen spinach, thawed and well drained
2 eggs
6 to 8 tablespoons flour
2 tablespoons milk
1/4 teaspoon freshly grated nutmeg
salt and freshly ground pepper to taste
vegetable oil for cooking

Prepare brains according to Steps I and II in basic instructions; coarsely chop. Combine with remaining ingredients and drop by spoonfuls into hot oil, 1/2 inch deep. Brown, turning to cook evenly. Drain on paper towels. Serve with grilled or sliced raw tomatoes. Good for brunch or a light supper. Serves 6

CANNELLONI STUFFED WITH BRAINS

Prepare brains according to Steps I and II in basic instructions, parboiling in a court bouillon (1 clove garlic and 2 tablespoons vinegar added to cooking liquid in addition to other ingredients). Then chop brains and sauté with onions and fresh tomatoes. Fill cooked cannelloni with this mixture, shredded lettuce, sliced radishes, sprigs of coriander and cold tomato sauce (page 133).

BRAINS & HAM FOO YUNG

1/2 pound brains (any kind)
8 tablespoons diced ham
4 eggs, beaten
6 ounces bean sprouts
2 small stalks celery, thinly sliced
2 tablespoons chopped spring onions
8 tablespoons chopped water chestnuts
1 tablespoon cornflour
1 tablespoon soy sauce
1/2 teaspoon fried sesame oil*
peanut oil for cooking

Prepare brains according to Steps I and II in basic instructions; let cool and chop very finely. Combine brains with ham, eggs and 2 tablespoons water; stir well. Then add remaining ingredients, blending well. Heat oil in a frying pan over medium heat. When hot, add brain mixture by half cupfuls to the pan, making 3-inch pancakes. Cook 2 to 3 minutes; turn when eggs begin to set and cook until golden. Keep pancakes warm until all mixture is used. Serve with soy sauce.
Makes 12 3-inch pancakes
*The dark seasoning oil available at Oriental stores.

BRAINS & SCRAMBLED EGGS

1/2 pound brains (any kind)
1 small carrot
2 sprigs parsley
1/2 teaspoon thyme
5 peppercorns
2 tablespoons finely chopped parsley
2 tablespoons chopped chives
dash of cayenne
salt and freshly ground pepper to taste
3 tablespoons butter
6 eggs
3 tablespoons cream

Prepare brains according to Steps I and II in basic instructions, adding carrot, parsley sprigs, thyme and peppercorns to cooking liquid. Pat brains dry and cut in small dice. Combine brains with chopped parsley, chives, cayenne, salt and pepper. Sauté over medium heat in butter until slightly golden. Combine eggs and cream with wire whisk and pour into pan. Reduce heat slightly, stir from bottom of pan, in a folding manner, and cook until eggs just begin to set. Place on a heated platter. Serve with crisp bacon, if desired. Boiled parsleyed potatoes and asparagus tips are also good accompaniments.
Serves 4

BRAINS AU BEURRE NOIR
(Brains in Black Butter)

1-1/2 pounds brains (any kind)
1/4 pound butter
4 tablespoons fresh lemon juice
2 tablespoons chopped parsley
2 tablespoons chopped chives
1/2 teaspoon freshly ground black pepper
2 tablespoons capers, drained

Prepare brains according to Steps I and II in basic instructions, parboiling in a court bouillon. Cut in thick slices and keep warm. Make a black butter sauce by melting butter over medium heat, cooking until browned well, but not burned. Add lemon juice, parsley, chives, pepper and capers; cook 2 minutes. Adjust seasonings. Pour over warm brains.
Serves 4

BRAIN FRITTERS

1 pound calf brains
2 tablespoons butter
1 tablespoon flour
4 tablespoons creamy milk
salt and freshly ground pepper to taste
1/4 teaspoon freshly grated nutmeg
1 egg white, beaten
8 tablespoons fine bread crumbs (or more)
vegetable oil for frying

Prepare brains according to Steps I and II in basic instructions, parboiling for 15 minutes; chop finely. Make binder by melting butter in saucepan. Then add flour; stir and cook for 3 to 5 minutes. Stir in milk and cook until smooth and thickened; cool. Combine with brains and add egg white and enough bread crumbs to form a ball. Shape into balls about the size of a walnut. Fry until golden brown in hot oil. Drain on paper towels.
Serves 4

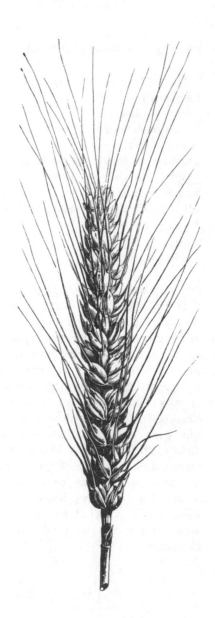

SAUTÉED BRAINS

Sautéing brains is the most classic of all brain preparations. It is always necessary to soak and clean brains; however, parboiling is optional. (Follow Step I in basic instructions.) Brains should be drained well and dried between paper towels before proceeding with recipes.
Season the brains with salt, freshly ground pepper and paprika and then roll in flour, bread crumbs or cornmeal. Sauté them in butter, oil, bacon fat or any combination thereof, until delicately browned. Deglaze pan with a little dry white wine, if desired. Serve with lemon wedges, Worcestershire sauce or tomato sauce.

Variations for added flavor: Rub some finely chopped garlic into brains before dusting with flour; or flavor butter, oil or bacon fat with a small sprig of fresh rosemary or sage; or sauté fresh sliced tomatoes or mushrooms in the same pan after sautéing brains, and serve with brains.

HERB-BAKED CALF BRAINS

1-1/2 pounds calf brains
5 peppercorns
2 tablespoons vinegar
1/2 teaspoon thyme
1 teaspoon salt
1/2 onion, sliced
4 sprigs parsley
1 bay leaf
1 egg
about 3 ounces flour
3 tablespoons butter
4 tablespoons lemon juice
2 tablespoons chopped chives
lemon wedges

Prepare brains according to Steps I and II in basic instructions, adding peppercorns, vinegar, thyme, salt, onion, parsley and bay leaf to cooking liquid. Bring to a gentle boil, reduce heat and cook for 15 minutes. Cool in liquid and drain.

Mix egg with 2 tablespoons water. Dip brain in egg, then in flour and brown in butter. Place in baking dish, sprinkle with lemon juice and scatter with chives. Bake at 375°F until golden, about 20 minutes. Garnish with lemon wedges.
Serves 4 to 6

KOHLRABIS STUFFED WITH BRAINS

Since kohlrabis are at the peak of their season during June and July, this would make a rather special first course for a summer dinner party. However, they are available until November, so this would also make a hearty and rich one-meal dish for one of the first crisp evenings of autumn.

8 young kohlrabis
1 pound calf brains
1/4 pound butter
1 small onion, chopped
salt and freshly ground pepper to taste
1/8 teaspoon freshly grated nutmeg
1 tablespoon chopped parsley
1 egg
1/2 pint sour cream

Carefully peel kohlrabis and hollow them out. Prepare brains according to Steps I and II in basic instructions; cut into small pieces. Heat half of the butter and sauté onions and brains 10 minutes; remove from heat. Add salt, pepper, nutmeg, parsley and egg; mix well. Stuff each kohlrabi with mixture. Place in a shallow baking dish and spoon sour cream evenly over them. Top with remaining butter. Bake in a 350°F oven for 30 minutes. Serve hot.
Serves 8 as a first course, 4 as an entrée

ROAST CHICKEN STUFFED WITH BRAINS

1 pound brains (any kind)
1 roasting chicken or large fryer, about 3 pounds
salt and freshly ground pepper
2 tablespoons olive oil
4 tablespoons dry white wine
1 tablespoon chopped parsley
2 tablespoons chopped spring onion
1 teaspoon fresh tarragon leaves, chopped
1/2 teaspoon salt
1/2 teaspoon coarsely ground pepper
softened butter as needed.

Prepare brains according to Step I in basic instructions; leave whole. Salt and pepper inside cavity of chicken. Combine remaining ingredients and marinate brains 1 hour, turning from time to time. Stuff chicken with brains, including marinade; truss with white string or skewer securely. Place chicken on a rack in a roasting tin and spread with soft butter. Roast in a 400°F oven for 1 hour, or longer, depending on size of bird. Remove brains carefully from cavity and serve along with chicken.
Serves 6 to 8

SWEETBREADS

PREPARATION OF SWEETBREADS

When selecting sweetbreads, be aware that there are 2 glands that are classified as sweetbreads. The first are the throat sweetbreads, or thymus gland, found in the neck of young mammals. These are elongated in shape and disappear as the animal matures. The other kind are the heart or belly sweetbreads. These are located close to the heart and are rounded or contoured. Most cooks prefer this variety for sautéing or braising, as they are more delicate. For the same reason, veal or lamb sweetbreads are preferred to beef sweetbreads. Veal or lamb sweetbreads may be recognized by their whiteness and tenderness; beef sweetbreads have a reddish cast and are somewhat resistant to thumb pressure. Freshness is a critical factor in selecting sweetbreads, as soft gland tissue deteriorates readily from exposure. Look for moist, plump sweetbreads. Sweetbreads should be cooked within a day of purchase.

Step I: Soaking
Soak sweetbreads in cold, even icy water, to cover, for 20 minutes.

Step II: Parboiling
Place sweetbreads in cold water to cover with 1/2 teaspoon salt and the juice of 1/2 lemon added to each 1-1/2 pints water. (Acidulated water helps retain whiteness.) Bring to a gentle boil, reduce heat and simmer for 15 minutes. Immediately plunge sweetbreads into cold water to firm up meat. Remove the tubes which connect the pair and the outer membranes; pat dry.
Note: A court bouillon also may be used for parboiling. Most often the sweetbreads are cooled in this stock for added flavor.

Ingredients for court bouillon:
1 small onion
1 stalk celery, with top
1 carrot
1/2 bay leaf
water to cover

Step III: Chilling
When sweetbreads are to be used for escalopes, after parboiling weight with a heavy plate to remove excess liquid. Place in the refrigerator for 1 to 2 hours; slice crosswise 1/4 inch thick and proceed with recipe.

SWEETBREAD SOUP WITH VERMICELLI

1 pair veal sweetbreads
2-1/2 pints rich beef or veal stock
1 tablespoon chopped parsley
4 ounces vermicelli
salt and freshly ground pepper

Prepare sweetbreads according to Step I in basic instructions. Then simmer in stock and parsley for 20 minutes. Remove sweetbreads and chop. Return to pot with vermicelli and season to taste with salt and pepper. Cook for 5 to 7 minutes.
Serves 4 to 6
Note: Brains may be substituted for sweetbreads in the above recipe. Prepare according to Step I in basic instructions for brains.

Variation: For a Yugoslavian touch, sieve sweetbreads. Then beat with 1 egg, 2 tablespoons lemon juice and 3 tablespoons yoghurt. Pour hot stock gradually into this mixture; return to heat for a minute or two. Do not boil.

SWEETBREADS & CUCUMBER SALAD

1/2 pound veal sweetbreads
8 tablespoons peeled and diced cucumber
1 stalk celery, diced
4 tablespoons chopped spring onions
1 large unpeeled apple, cored and diced
4 tablespoons sour cream
4 tablespoons mayonnaise
1 teaspoon sugar
chopped walnuts for garnish

Prepare sweetbreads according to Steps I and II in basic instructions; dice, making about 1 cup and chill thoroughly. Place in bowl and add chilled vegetables and apples; mix lightly. Make dressing by combining remaining ingredients. Toss lightly into sweetbread mixture. Serve on lettuce leaves, garnished with walnuts.
Serves 4

Variation: Follow the above recipe, chopping all ingredients finely. Use for a spread on open-face sandwiches.

BAKED SWEETBREADS

1 pound veal or lamb sweetbreads
4 tablespoons melted butter
1 clove garlic, finely chopped
1/2 teaspoon salt
dash of white pepper
2 tablespoons fine bread crumbs

Prepare sweetbreads according to Steps I and II in basic instructions, parboiling just 5 minutes. Split crosswise. Dip pieces in butter mixed with garlic; season with salt and pepper. Place in shallow baking dish, spoon over remaining garlic butter, sprinkle with bread crumbs and bake in a 350°F oven for 40 minutes.
Serves 2

Variation: Equal parts of bread crumbs and freshly grated Parmesan cheese may be substituted for plain bread crumbs. Also 1/2 teaspoon chopped chives and 1/2 teaspoon tarragon may be added to bread crumbs for a spicier flavor.

DEEP-FRIED OR SAUTÉED SWEETBREADS

1 pound veal or lamb sweetbreads
1/2 teaspoon salt·
1/4 teaspoon white pepper
1/8 teaspoon powdered ginger
6 to 8 tablespoons fine bread crumbs
1 egg, beaten
vegetable oil for frying, or
butter for sautéing

Prepare sweetbreads according to Steps I and II in basic instructions, parboiling for 10 minutes only. Cut in 1/2-inch slices. Combine bread crumbs with seasonings. Roll sweetbreads in crumbs, dip in egg and roll once again in crumbs. Fry in hot oil, 1/2 inch deep, or sauté in butter until lightly browned.
Serves 2

GRILLED SWEETBREADS

For grilled sweetbreads, follow the preceding recipe, placing sweetbreads on rack of grilling pan. Grill for about 14 minutes, turning once. Serve with lemon wedges or Hollandaise sauce, fried bacon, a grilled tomato and green salad. Grilled mushroom caps are another good garnish.

ESCALOPES OF SWEETBREADS WITH HAM & CHEESE

1 pound veal sweetbreads
1/2 pound thinly sliced boiled ham
about 1/4 pound mild Cheddar cheese, grated
salt and freshly ground pepper
1/4 teaspoon freshly grated nutmeg

Prepare sweetbreads according to Steps I, II and III in basic instructions; slice crosswise 1/4 inch thick. Layer sweetbreads in shallow, buttered baking dish. Top first with ham slices, then with grated cheese. Season each layer with salt, pepper and nutmeg. Place in a 450°F oven and bake 15 minutes, until cheese is melted and slightly golden. Serve on hot or toasted French bread with a green salad and vinaigrette dressing.
Serves 2 to 3
Note: This is a good filling for crêpes.

SWEETBREAD CROQUETTES

1 pair veal sweetbreads, cooked and finely chopped
3 tablespoons butter
1-1/2 teaspoons flour
1/4 pint single cream
1 egg yolk, beaten
12 button mushrooms
1-1/2 teaspoons salt
1/4 teaspoon white pepper
1 teaspoon finely chopped parsley
1/2 teaspoon onion juice
beaten eggs
fine bread crumbs
vegetable oil

Prepare sweetbreads according to Steps I and II in basic instructions, parboiling them in acidulated water or court bouillon. Heat 1 tablespoon butter in a saucepan and add flour, making a roux; add cream, stirring until smooth. Add egg yolk and sweetbreads; cook 1 minute. Remove from heat.

In the meantime, heat 2 tablespoons butter in a separate frying pan. Sauté mushrooms quickly; remove and finely chop. Add to sweetbread mixture, along with salt, pepper, parsley and onion juice; mix well. Shape into balls about the size of a walnut, roll in beaten eggs, then into bread crumbs. Fry in deep hot oil.
Serves 4

BRAISED SWEETBREADS & ONIONS

1 pound veal or lamb sweetbreads
3 tablespoons butter
2 tablespoons oil
2 onions, thinly sliced
1 teaspoon flour
dash of cayenne
1-1/2 teaspoons Worcestershire sauce
1 tablespoon tomato paste
2 tablespoons dry sherry
1/4 pint chicken stock

Prepare sweetbreads according to Steps I and II in basic instructions; slice. Heat 2 tablespoons butter and 1 tablespoon oil in a frying pan. Sauté sweetbreads until lightly browned. Remove and keep warm. Add remaining butter and oil and onions, and sauté until golden. Sprinkle with flour and stir well; add remaining ingredients. Simmer for 5 minutes. Return sweetbreads to sauce and continue cooking another 15 minutes. Serve with rice or boiled noodles or on toast.
Serves 2 to 4

Variation: Follow the above recipe, omitting tomato paste and onions. Add 2 large carrots, finely grated, and 1/2 teaspoon tarragon to the pan immediately after sautéing sweetbreads.

SWEETBREADS & SCALLOPS

1 pair veal sweetbreads
4 tablespoons butter
2 ounces mushrooms, sliced
3/4 pound scallops, quartered
4 tablespoons flour
1/2 pint milk
4 tablespoons double cream
4 tablespoons dry sherry or vermouth
salt and white pepper to taste
buttered bread crumbs

Prepare sweetbreads according to Steps I and II in basic instructions; cut in pieces. Heat butter and sauté mushrooms and scallops for 5 minutes; remove with slotted spoon. Add flour, making a roux; add milk and cream stirring constantly, until smooth and slightly thickened. Add sherry and salt and pepper. Return scallops, mushrooms and sweetbreads to sauce. Pour into individual casseroles and sprinkle with buttered bread crumbs. Bake in a 350°F oven for 20 minutes. Garnish with watercress.
Serves 4

Variation: Follow the above recipe, substituting oysters for scallops.

ESCALOPES OF SWEETBREADS & ASPARAGUS

1 pound veal sweetbreads
1 egg, beaten
fine bread crumbs
2 to 4 tablespoons clarified butter
salt and freshly ground pepper
4 tablespoons dry white wine
1 pound asparagus tips, steamed
    just until tender
melted butter and lemon juice

Prepare sweetbreads according to Steps I, II and III in basic instructions; slice crosswise 1/4-inch thick. Dip sweetbreads in egg, then into bread crumbs; sauté in butter until delicately browned. Season to taste. Place in circle around serving platter; keep warm. Deglaze pan with wine and pour over sweetbreads. Place asparagus in center of platter and drizzle with melted butter and lemon juice. Serve with fried potatoes.
Serves 2 to 3

Variation: Follow the above recipe, substituting buttered egg noodles or a saffron-flavored pilaf for the asparagus. Serve with a green salad.

SWEETBREADS & VEAL KIDNEYS

1 pair veal sweetbreads
3 veal kidneys, cut in small pieces
6 tablespoons butter
6 tablespoons oil
4 tablespoons very finely chopped shallots, or
8 tablespoons finely chopped spring onions
salt and white pepper
1/2 pound button mushrooms
5 tablespoons Madeira
1 teaspoon tarragon
1 teaspoon cornflour, mixed with
2 tablespoons reserved stock
chopped parsley

Prepare sweetbreads according to Steps I and II, parboiling in court bouillon; reserve cooking liquid. Cut in small pieces. Heat 3 tablespoons each butter and oil, and sauté shallots until transparent; add sweetbreads and sauté 5 minutes longer. Salt and pepper to taste. Remove to serving dish and keep warm. Add remaining butter and oil to the pan and sauté kidneys. Add mushrooms and sauté 5 minutes. Season to taste. Remove to serving dish and keep warm. Deglaze pan with Madeira, 1 cup reserved stock and tarragon. Bring to a boil; thicken juices with cornflour mixture, stirring constantly, until smooth. Pour over meats and sprinkle with chopped parsley. Serve with rice, in vol-au-vent cases or on buttered toast.
Serves 6

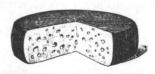

SWEETBREAD SOUFFLÉ

1/2 pound cooked veal sweetbreads, finely chopped
3 tablespoons butter
3 tablespoons flour
scant 1/2 pint creamy milk
3 eggs, separated
1/2 teaspoon white pepper
salt
dash of nutmeg
4 tablespoons grated Gruyère cheese
freshly grated Parmesan cheese

Sweetbreads should be prepared according to Steps I and II in basic instructions, parboiling in a court bouillon (for added flavor).
Preheat oven to 425°F. Heat butter in saucepan; add flour, making a roux. Add milk, stirring constantly, until smooth and thickened. Stir in beaten egg yolks, sweetbreads and seasonings. Allow to cool slightly, add Gruyère.
In the meantime, beat egg whites until stiff, but not dry. Butter a 2-1/2-pint soufflé dish and dust well with Parmesan cheese. Stir 1/3 of beaten egg whites into sweetbread mixture. Then fold remaining egg whites carefully into mixture. Pour into prepared soufflé dish and put in oven. Immediately reduce heat to 375°F and cook for 17 to 20 minutes for a French-type soufflé (with a soft center). For a drier soufflé, cook 30 minutes. This is beautiful served as a first course or luncheon entrée.
Serves 4

Variation: Brains may be substituted for sweetbreads. Prepare according to Steps I and II of basic instructions for brains.

SWEETBREADS SMOTHERED IN VEGETABLES

3 pairs veal or lamb sweetbreads
3 tablespoons butter
1 onion, sliced
1 carrot, sliced
1 stalk celery, sliced
1 bay leaf
1/2 teaspoon thyme
2 sprigs parsley
1 teaspoon flour
salt and freshly ground pepper
1/4 pint dry white wine
6 ounces fresh peas
2 tablespoons Madeira

Prepare sweetbreads according to Steps I and II in basic instructions, parboiling in court bouillon for 5 minutes only; divide in pieces; reserve cooking liquid. Heat butter in a flameproof casserole and sauté vegetables for 10 minutes until lightly browned. Stir in seasonings and flour. Salt and pepper sweetbreads and lay on top of vegetables. Add wine and 1/2 pint reserved stock; bring to a boil. Cover immediately and place in a preheated 350°F oven for 1 hour, adjusting temperature so the ingredients are barely simmering. Baste from time to time. During last 10 minutes of cooking period, add peas and Madeira. Adjust seasonings. Serve with French bread.
Serves 6

CREAMED SWEETBREADS

1 pound veal sweetbreads
4 tablespoons butter
4 tablespoons flour
1/2 pint chicken stock, or
part dry white wine and stock
1/2 pint milk
1/2 teaspoon tarragon
dash of freshly grated nutmeg
salt and white pepper to taste

Prepare sweetbreads according to Steps I and II in basic instructions. Divide them up into pieces. Heat butter in a saucepan; add flour, making a roux. Gradually add stock and milk, stirring constantly, until smooth and thickened. Add seasonings. Then add sweetbreads and heat through. Serve on fried bread rounds, on toast, in vol-au-vent cases or over steamed white rice.
Serves 4

Variations: Pour over and/or fill omelettes and garnish with chopped chives; or omit tarragon and add 1 teaspoon grated orange peel to sauce; or add 8 tablespoons sliced water chestnuts just before serving; or sprinkle toasted almonds or crumbled bacon over sweetbreads just before serving; or reduce sweetbreads to 1/2 pound, dice them and add 1/2 pound diced cooked chicken; or add 8 tablespoons grated Emmenthal cheese to the sauce and sprinkle finished dish with freshly grated Parmesan cheese.

SWEETBREAD & VEAL PATTIES

1 pair veal sweetbreads
1 pound minced veal
salt and freshly ground pepper to taste
2 tablespoons finely chopped spring onions
2 tablespoons finely chopped parsley
1 clove garlic, finely chopped (optional)
1 egg, beaten
2 tablespoons each butter and olive oil

Prepare sweetbreads according to Steps I and II in basic instructions, parboiling in court bouillon 10 minutes only; chop finely. Add sweetbreads to minced veal and mix with salt, pepper, spring onions, parsley, garlic and egg. Form into patties and brown in hot butter and oil. Serve on split French rolls with sliced tomatoes, onions, pickles and olives.

Makes 4 to 6 patties

Variations: Follow the above recipe, substituting either minced chicken, turkey or beef for the veal.

Follow the above recipe, adding 12 to 18 mushrooms to pan after browning meat patties. Deglaze pan with 2 to 3 tablespoons Madeira and pour over all. Garnish with either parsley sprigs or watercress.

Follow the above recipe, serving crisp fried bacon with the patties. Serve with a green salad dressed with vinaigrette and crusty bread.

SWEETBREADS WRAPPED IN BACON

1-1/2 pounds lamb or veal sweetbreads
freshly ground pepper
3/4 pound bacon rashers, derinded and
    blanched in water 5 minutes
1 onion, chopped
3 large tomatoes, peeled and sliced
1 teaspoon chopped fresh sweet basil
    or parsley
6 to 8 tablespoons fine bread crumbs

Prepare sweetbreads according to Steps I and II in basic instructions, parboiling in court bouillon; reserve cooking liquid. Cut in uniform pieces, about 1-1/2 x 1 inch; pepper lightly. Wrap each sweetbread piece with a strip of bacon and place in a baking dish, seam side down. Place onions, then tomatoes on top. Sprinkle with basil. Pour 1/2 pint reserved liquid over all and sprinkle with fine bread crumbs. Bake in a 350°F oven for 40 minutes, until meat is tender. Serve with browned or boiled potatoes or boiled cabbage.
Serves 4 to 6

SWEETBREAD & OYSTER PIE

1 pound veal sweetbreads
12 oysters or small scallops, halved
2 hard-boiled eggs, sliced
3 ounces mushrooms, sliced and
    sautéed in
3 tablespoons butter
generous 1/2 pint Béchamel sauce
    (page 133)
4 tablespoons Madeira or dry sherry
1/4 teaspoon freshly grated nutmeg
1/8 teaspoon cayenne
2 tablespoons chopped parsley
1/2 teaspoon salt
1/2 teaspoon white pepper
scone dough for 10-inch pie
    (recipe follows)
1 egg beaten with
2 tablespoons milk

Prepare sweetbreads according to Steps I and II in basic instructions, parboiling in court bouillon; slice. Layer sweetbreads, oysters, hard-boiled eggs and sautéed mushrooms in a buttered 2-1/2-pint baking dish. Combine remaining ingredients and pour over all.
Roll out dough 1/4 inch thick on a floured board. Cut a 1-1/2-inch-wide strip and fit around rim of baking dish; cut top pastry in a round, 3/4 inch wider in diameter than baking dish. Brush rim with egg mixture and fit with top pastry. Pinch or flute edges together. Prick top well to allow steam to evaporate during baking period. Brush top with egg mixture to glaze. Bake in a 375°F oven for 45 minutes, or until pastry is golden.
Serves 4 to 6

SCONE DOUGH

6 ounces flour (unbleached if possible)
2 teaspoons baking powder
1/2 teaspoon salt
1-1/2 ounces butter
3 tablespoons vegetable oil
1 egg, beaten

Sift flour, baking powder and salt together. Cut in butter; add oil and egg. Form into a ball, adding a little cold water if dough is stiff. Roll out 1/4 inch thick. Use for top crust of pot pies or deep-dish pies.
Makes 1 10-inch top crust

TONGUE

Although tongue has been a popular folk food throughout the ages, it achieved its fame during the days of the Roman Empire. When snobbism and a penchant for ostentatious spending became the way of life, the Romans began to serve only the tongues of songbirds. The intrepid gourmet, Apicius, maintained that flamingo tongues were a great delicacy.

In France in the 1300's, the first official inspection of meat transpired with the examination of pig tongues for ulcers which were thought to be the cause of leprosy. The inspectors, in fact, became known as *langueyeurs* (derived from the French *langue,* meaning tongue).

The 15th-century Italian banquet often included tongue in one form or another for it was thought to be both flavorful and wholesome. We've seen recipes for salted pork tongues cooked in wine and for pickled tongue — chopped with parsley, mint, sage, spices and drowned in vinegar. Whale tongues were eaten in 16th century France. The common people of the coastal regions braised them with lentils or peas, whereas the bourgeoisie preferred theirs spit-roasted. French gastronome de la Reynière writes of carp tongue in the 19th century. Evidently, when carp was served, the presentation began by cutting off its head. The head was always served to the most distinguished guest at the table because it contained the choicest morsel of all—the tongue! Another of his renowned colleagues, Beauvilliers, goes into raptures over a ragout of carp tongues laced with sauce italienne.

In America in the early 1800's, buffalo tongues were used by the Indians in bartering for whiskey from the settlers. In fact, there is one incident recorded where a band of Sioux traded 1400 buffalo tongues for a few gallons of whiskey. Actually, anywhere you find herdsmen — the Pyrenees, Australia, South America, Mexico — you will find tongue used abundantly in cooking.

PREPARATION OF BEEF (OX), CALF, LAMB AND PORK TONGUE

Step I: Cleaning

Soak tongue in cold water to cover for 1 hour. One tablespoon vinegar or lemon juice may be added for each 1-1/2 pints water. Drain, discarding water. Some cooks prefer to eliminate this step and instead only rinse the tongues under cold, running water.

Step II: Parboiling for Calf, Lamb and Pork Tongues

Place tongue in a large pot, adding fresh water to cover, salting lightly. Parboil, uncovered, 10 minutes for small tongues and up to 30 minutes for larger ones, or until skins may be removed easily. Drain, remove skin and proceed with recipe. (Plunging a parboiled tongue in cold water makes the skin easier to remove.)

Step III: Court Bouillon for Beef (Ox) Tongues

Place tongue in large pot, adding the following court bouillon to cover. Simmer, covered, for 2 to 3 hours, or until tender. Drain and cool slightly, or allow to cool in stock for added flavor. Remove skin, gristle and excess fat from the base of the tongue. Proceed with recipes, or wrap well and refrigerate or freeze. The reserved stock may be strained and used as a soup base.

Ingredients for court bouillon:
1 onion, stuck with 2 cloves if
    desired
1 bay leaf
1 carrot
1/2 lemon (optional)
6 to 8 peppercorns
2 stalks celery, with tops
3 to 4 sprigs parsley
water to cover

CORNED OR PICKLED TONGUE

2 ox tongues, or
5 pounds veal, lamb or pork tongues
pickling brine (page 132)

Wash and soak tongues in cold water to cover for 10 minutes. Place in earthenware crock or glass jar and pour in cooled brine to cover tongues. Weight with a heavy plate or clean piece of wood to keep tongues completely submerged in brine. Cover crock with loose-fitting lid or with cheesecloth. Set in a cool place 2 to 5 days, depending on variety of tongue selected and degree of pickling desired. (The longer the tongues are kept in the brine, the saltier they become.)
Prepare tongue in court bouillon according to Step III in basic instructions, adding additional herbs if desired. Bring to a boil, reduce heat, cover and simmer for 1 hour for veal, lamb or pork tongues, 2 to 3 hours for beef tongues. Always check to see if meat is tender before removing from heat. Skin and serve.
Note: Tongue may be soaked overnight in cold water to remove excessive saltiness before cooking in court bouillon.

IDEAS FOR COOKED TONGUE

• Substitute tongue for ham in a "Reuben" sandwich. Spread mustard on slices of rye bread, then layer with tongue, sauerkraut and Emmenthal cheese. Butter outer sides of bread and toast gently or grill until cheese has melted and both sides are crisp.
• Layer slices of tongue, avocado and Spanish onion on French or whole-grain bread. Spread slices of bread with mayonnaise and add alfalfa sprouts if desired.

• Layer tongue and creamed cheese or sour cream flavored with dill on whole-grain bread. Garnish with capers.
• Make croque-monsieur, using tongue. Butter outer sides of bread, then fill with a slice of Emmenthal cheese, a slice of tongue, strips of pimiento and another slice of Emmenthal cheese. Grill or fry gently until cheese has melted and both sides are golden brown.
• Cut tongue into strips and toss in in green salad of watercress or spinach and crispy bacon bits. Dress with a vinaigrette.
• Combine chopped tongue with grated onion, chopped celery and cooked rice. Bind with a little mayonnaise, flavored with lemon juice, salt and pepper. Good stuffed into tomatoes for a first course.
• Tongue is good combined with turkey, chicken, ham and/or corned beef. Use in a chef's salad dressed with a vinaigrette or Roquefort dressing.
• Combine diced tongue with cooked cauliflowerets, sliced avocado and chopped sweet red peppers. Serve with an olive oil and lemon juice vinaigrette and pile into lettuce cups.
• Chopped tongue makes a good filling for burritos (page 81).

SAUCES FOR TONGUE

There are numerous sauces, both hot and cold, that may be served with tongue. In most cases, both smoked tongue or plain boiled tongue may be used—the choice is your preference.

COLD CUCUMBER SAUCE

1/2 pint mayonnaise
1/2 pint double cream, whipped
1 to 2 tablespoons lemon juice
1/4 teaspoon salt
2 to 3 cucumbers, peeled, seeded and finely diced
2 teaspoons fresh chopped dill

Fold mayonnaise and whipped cream together. Stir in lemon juice and salt; then fold in cucumbers and dill. Chill well. Serve on cold sliced tongue, smoked, pickled or plain.
Makes about 1-1/2 pints

WATERCRESS MAYONNAISE

1/2 pint mayonnaise, or
1/4 pint each mayonnaise and sour cream
2 tablespoons lemon juice
2 to 3 ounces watercress, coarsely chopped
1 teaspoon sugar

Place all ingredients in blender and purée until smooth. Serve on cold sliced tongue.
Makes about 3/4 pint

ITALIAN SWEET & SOUR SAUCE

1 carrot, cut up
1 onion, cut up
1 ounce bitter chocolate, in pieces
1/2 pint stock (reserved tongue stock preferred)
3 tablespoons butter
generous 1/4 pint wine vinegar
1 tablespoon cornflour
6 to 8 tablespoons raisins
6 to 8 tablespoons chopped pitted prunes
6 to 8 tablespoons pine nuts
2 tablespoons diced candied fruit
1 tablespoon sugar

Purée carrot, onion, chocolate and stock in a blender. Heat in saucepan with butter; cook, over moderate heat, 10 minutes. Combine wine vinegar with cornflour and add to saucepan. Then add remaining ingredients and simmer another 10 minutes. Add slices of tongue and warm through.
Serves 6 to 8

TONGUE

CHILI SAUCE

1 onion, chopped
1 clove garlic
1 pound ripe tomatoes, peeled and
    chopped
1/2 teaspoon cumin
salt and freshly ground pepper
1 or 2 dried red chilis, or
1 or 2 teaspoons compound chili
    powder
2 tablespoons olive oil

Purée onion, garlic and tomatoes in
blender. Add cumin, salt, pepper and
chilis. Heat oil in a frying pan. Add
tomato mixture; simmer 10 minutes.
Place slices of tongue on flameproof
platter, pour sauce over all and simmer
a few minutes to heat through. Hot
tortillas (page 134) and a salad of lettuce, fresh coriander, olives and
radishes would be great accompaniments for this dish.
Serves 6

PORT & CRANBERRY SAUCE

1/4 pint cranberry sauce
1/4 pint Port
1/2 pint orange juice
1/2 large lemon, cut in thin slices
4 to 6 gingersnaps, dissolved in
    orange juice
1/8 teaspoon ground cloves, or to taste

Combine all ingredients in a saucepan
and simmer for 10 minutes. Pour over
slices of tongue and heat in a 350°F
oven for a few minutes. Serve with
brown or wild rice.
Serves 6 to 8

ONION SAUCE

2 onions, thinly sliced
1 teaspoon sugar
3 tablespoons butter
3 tablespoons flour
3/4 pint beef stock
3 to 4 tablespoons dry vermouth
salt and freshly ground pepper to taste

Gently sauté onions with sugar in butter for 15 minutes, carmelizing
slightly. Add flour, stirring in well, and
cook for 5 minutes. Then add stock,
vermouth and seasonings; simmer for
10 minutes.
Place slices of tongue in baking dish,
pour sauce over all and bake, uncovered, 25 minutes in a 350°F oven. Serve
with freshly boiled egg noodles, a
green salad or cucumber and tomatoes.
Serves 6

HORSERADISH SAUCE

1/2 pint stock (reserved tongue
stock preferred)
2 tablespoons freshly grated
horseradish
2 tablespoons butter
1 tablespoon fine bread crumbs
4 to 5 tablespoons double cream
2 egg yolks, beaten
1 teaspoon Dijon-style mustard
salt and freshly ground pepper to taste

Simmer stock and horseradish in a
saucepan for 15 minutes. Remove
from heat and stir in butter, bread
crumbs and cream. Return to low
heat, stirring until it begins to thicken.
Slowly add egg yolks, stirring all the
while. Add mustard, salt and pepper.
Pour over warm tongue slices. Serve
with parsleyed potatoes and dill pickles.
Serves 6

SPANISH ALMOND SAUCE

2 tablespoons olive oil
1 clove garlic, finely chopped
1/2 pound ripe tomatoes, peeled and
chopped
2 tablespoons chopped green olives
4 tablespoons chopped blanched
almonds
8 tablespoons stock (reserved tongue
stock preferred)
2 tablespoons bread crumbs
capers for garnish

Heat oil in sauté pan and cook garlic
until softened. Add tomatoes, olives
and almonds; cook 5 minutes. Add
stock and thicken with bread crumbs.
Add slices of cooked tongue and heat
through. Garnish with capers.
Serves 6

WALNUT & PEANUT SAUCE

2 or more fresh hot green chilis, seeded
2 ounces walnuts
2 ounces peanuts
1/8 teaspoon ground cloves
1/4 teaspoon cinnamon
1 onion, chopped
1 clove garlic
4 tablespoons bread crumbs
3 tablespoons peanut oil
3/4 pint stock (reserved tongue
stock preferred)
salt and freshly ground pepper to taste

Purée chilis, walnuts, peanuts, spices,
onion, garlic and bread crumbs in
blender. Heat oil in frying pan. Add
purée; cook 5 minutes. Add stock, salt
and pepper and cook until slightly
thickened. Add slices of tongue and
heat through.
Serves 6

TONGUE EN GELÉE

1 whole ox tongue, cooked and skinned
1 tablespoon powdered gelatine
3/4 pint lightly jellied beef consommé
2 tablespoons dry sherry
julienne-cut strips of pimiento,
    cooked carrots and green beans,
slices of hard-boiled egg and olives
    as needed

Drain and weight tongue (with a heavy plate) overnight in the refrigerator to remove excess moisture. Chill vegetables. Dissolve gelatine in 2 tablespoons cold water. Add to consommé and melt over low heat; add sherry and cool until partially set. Paint a layer of consommé over tongue; chill. Paint decorations with some of the partially set consommé. Place decorations on tongue as desired. Repeat painting of entire tongue several times. Pour remaining consommé into a shallow dish; chill and dice. To serve tongue, garnish with watercress and surround with diced consommé.

TONGUE IN ASPIC

2   tablespoons powdered gelatine
4 tablespoons dry white wine
1/2 pint tomato juice
3/4 pint clear stock (tongue stock
    preferred)
6 to 8 tablespoons seeded, chopped
    cucumber
3 tablespoons chopped green pepper
1/2 pound cooked tongue (any kind),
    finely diced
1 teaspoon chopped fresh basil, or
1/2 teaspoon dried basil
freshly ground pepper to taste

Soften gelatine in wine. Heat, stirring, until dissolved. Add tomato juice and stock; refrigerate until partially set. Combine remaining ingredients with partially set gelatine. Pour into a deep, 2-1/2 pint dish. Chill until set. Turn out and serve on a bed of watercress, accompanied by a lemon mayonnaise or sour cream.
Serves 6 to 8

TONGUE MOUSSE

1 pound minced cooked tongue
  (any kind)
2 tablespoons powdered gelatine
4 tablespoons cold water
3/4 pint beef bouillon
6 tablespoons mayonnaise
1 teaspoon Dijon-style mustard
2 teaspoons Worcestershire sauce
4 tablespoons grated onion
2 tablespoons finely chopped parsley
2 tablespoons lemon juice
2 teaspoons fresh chopped dill
dash of cayenne
1/4 pint double cream, whipped

Soften gelatine in cold water. Bring bouillon to a boil; add to gelatine and stir until dissolved. Chill until partially set. Combine meat with mayonnaise, mustard, Worcestershire, onion, parsley, lemon juice, dill and cayenne. Add to gelatine mixture. Then fold whipped cream into meat mixture. Pour into lightly oiled 1-1/2-pint mould. Chill until set. Turn out on a bed of crisp lettuce leaves. Serve with horseradish sauce (following).
Serves 6 to 8.

HORSERADISH-SOUR CREAM SAUCE

1/2 pint sour cream
4 to 6 tablespoons mayonnaise
2 tablespoons prepared horseradish
pinch of sugar

Combine all ingredients and mix well.

TONGUE-STUFFED EGGS

4 tablespoons chopped celeriac
8 large eggs, hard-boiled
1/4 pound chopped boiled or smoked
  tongue (any kind)
scant 1/2 pint mayonnaise
4 tablespoons finely chopped gherkins
1 teaspoon dry mustard
salt and freshly ground pepper to taste

Parboil chopped celeriac for 2 minutes. Drain and cool. Cut eggs in half lengthwise; remove yolks. Combine yolks with remaining ingredients in a mixing bowl; mix well. Stuff into egg-white halves.
Makes 16 appetizers

TONGUE PASTIES

3/4 pound cooked tongue (any kind),
  very finely chopped
6 to 8 tablespoons single cream
1 egg white, beaten
1/2 teaspoon white pepper
rich shortcrust pastry for 2-crust pie
  (page 134)
1 egg yolk, lightly beaten with
1 tablespoon water

Combine the tongue, cream, egg white and pepper. Roll out pastry dough 1/8 inch thick and cut in 2-1/2-inch circles. Place about 1 tablespoon filling on each circle and fold over to form half moon; press edges together with tines of a fork. Brush with egg-yolk mixture. Place on an ungreased cookie sheet in a 375°F oven for 15 minutes, or until golden
Makes 18 to 24 pasties
Note: Greek filo dough may also be used with this filling. Cut it into 2x12-inch strips and brush with melted butter. Place a small spoonful of filling onto lower corner of strip. Begin folding into triangles, in flag-folding style, brushing with melted butter as you are folding; brush completed triangle with butter. Place on greased baking sheet in a 400°F oven for 15 to 20 minutes, or until puffed and golden brown.

29

PICKLED LAMB TONGUES

8 to 10 lamb tongues
2 to 3 sprigs parsley
2 teaspoons tarragon
1 bay leaf
1 tablespoon salt
14 peppercorns
1 onion, sliced
2 cloves garlic
4 whole allspice berries
1/4 pint white wine vinegar
1/4 pint water
salt to taste

Clean tongues and put into large stock pot with parsley, 1 teaspoon of the tarragon, bay leaf, salt, 8 of the peppercorns, onion, garlic and water to cover. Bring to a boil; reduce heat, cover and simmer about 1 hour, or until just tender. Drain and skin tongues (they will feel hot to the touch). Cut in half lengthwise. Place in crock or jar.
Combine remaining tarragon and peppercorns, allspice, vinegar, water and salt to taste in a small saucepan; boil 1 minute. Pour over peeled lamb tongues in crock. Let cool. Then store in refrigerator overnight to allow flavors to blend. Excellent served as a first course or on a country buffet table with mustard or horseradish.

HASH BROWN POTATOES & TONGUE

An old American favorite with a new twist. Keep the accompaniments traditional—eggs sunny-side up or poached, maybe a grilled tomato. All would be hearty fare for a Sunday brunch or supper.

2 rashers bacon, chopped
1 pound cooked tongue (any kind), diced
about 2 pounds potatoes, cooked and coarsely grated
1 onion, finely chopped
salt and freshly ground pepper to taste

Brown bacon in a frying pan until crisp. Remove bacon pieces to drain on paper towel; bacon fat remains in the pan. Combine cooked bacon, tongue, potatoes and onion; add to frying pan and press evenly over the surface. Cook over medium heat until golden brown on underside. Carefully turn over and brown top side. Slide onto warm platter; sprinkle with salt and pepper. Serve with eggs.
Serves 4

LAMB TONGUES VINAIGRETTE

8 lamb tongues
vinaigrette (page 132)
1 hard-boiled finely sieved egg
    for garnish

Prepare lamb tongues according to Steps I and III in basic instructions, simmering them in the court bouillon for only 1 hour; remove skin and split lengthwise. Place in bowl and pour vinaigrette over all. Marinate in refrigerator for 12 to 24 hours, turning from time to time. Arrange tongues on platter and garnish with egg before serving.

TONGUE IN THE POT

1 ox tongue, about 3 pounds
1 pound marrow bones, cut in
   1-1/2-inch pieces
1 clove garlic
1/2 teaspoon rosemary
6 turnips, scraped and cut in chunks
6 carrots, scraped and cut in chunks
12 button onions
6 to 8 new potatoes
6 whole leeks, white parts only
salt and freshly ground pepper to taste

Prepare tongue according to Steps I and III in basic instructions, adding marrow bones, garlic and rosemary to court bouillon and omitting lemon. Remove any scum that forms on top. Add vegetables during the last 45 minutes of cooking period. Remove tongue and skin; cut in 1/2-inch slices. Remove vegetables and marrow bones with a slotted spoon. Place tongue slices on a warm serving platter, surrounded by the vegetables and the marrow bones, if desired. Serve with small dishes of horseradish, mustard and gherkins. Strain the broth and serve in cups separately.
Serves 6

TONGUE & SPINACH ROLLS

12 thin slices cooked ox tongue
1 pound fresh spinach or 12 ounces
   frozen spinach, cooked and chopped
1 tablespoon butter, melted
salt and freshly ground pepper to taste
pinch of nutmeg
1 tablespoon prepared horseradish
1 teaspoon Dijon-style mustard
6 fluid ounces double cream

Combine spinach, butter, salt, pepper and nutmeg. Place a spoonful of the mixture on each tongue slice and roll up, securing with toothpicks. Place rolls in a buttered casserole. Combine horseradish, mustard and cream and pour over all. Bake in a preheated 400°F oven for 20 minutes.
Serves 4

BEEF TONGUE
EN PAPILLOTE

1 ox tongue
3 tablespoons butter
2 tablespoons finely chopped parsley
2 tablespoons finely chopped chives
1/2 teaspoon tarragon, bruised
4 large mushrooms, finely chopped
1/2 pound cooked chicken, chopped
2 tablespoons dry sherry
2 tablespoons tomato paste
6 slices prosciutto or Westphalian ham
watercress sprigs for garnish

Prepare tongue according to Steps I and III in basic instructions. Then slice tongue diagonally in 6 1/2-inch-thick slices, trying to obtain the largest possible slice. (Use leftover tongue in recipes called for minced, cooked tongue.) Heat butter and sauté parsley, chives, tarragon, mushrooms and chicken meat for 5 minutes, browning slightly. Add sherry and tomato paste and blend well. Cool mixture slightly. Spread herb-chicken mixture on each slice of tongue. Cover with prosciutto and place each of the prepared tongue slices on a piece of buttered parchment (brown paper may be substituted), fold and seal edges by turning under. Put on a buttered shallow baking dish and bake in a 350°F oven for 30 minutes. For serving, place papillotes on a heated serving platter and cut away upper layer of paper with a sharp knife. Garnish with watercress and serve with grilled tomato halves.
Serves 6

Variation: Follow the above recipe, substituting 8 tablespoons well-drained chopped spinach and 8 tablespoons cooked, minced veal for the chicken.

FEIJOADA

This dish probably more than any other, has made Brazilian cooking internationally known. Although we've used tongue, salt pork and chorizo, any number of meats may be added from pigs' tails to pork cutlets.

1 ox tongue, about 3 pounds
1 pound dried black beans
   (or red kidney beans)
1/2 pound salt pork, blanched
   2 minutes and diced
1 bay leaf
1 teaspoon crushed oregano
1/2 pound chorizo sausage, sliced
4 tablespoons lard
2 cloves garlic, finely chopped
1 onion, chopped
1 or more dried hot red chilis, crushed
1 tablespoon grated orange rind
orange slices

Prepare tongue according to Step I in basic instructions. Wash and soak beans overnight. Drain, discarding water. Return beans to pot with water to cover, salt pork, bay leaf, oregano and tongue; simmer, covered, 1-1/2 hours. Then add chorizo and continue cooking 30 minutes longer. When tongue is tender, remove from pot, skin and slice thinly. Drain beans, reserving liquid.

Heat lard and sauté garlic, onion and chili until onions are transparent. Add drained beans; mash and fry, adding more lard and reserved liquid if necessary to keep beans from drying out. Fry over low heat for 30 minutes or more. Place beans in center of heated platter and surround with tongue slices and chorizo. Garnish with grated orange rind and orange slices. Serve with tortillas (page 134) and a bowl of hot tomato sauce (page 133).
Serves 8

CHILI-TONGUE RELLENOS

8 strips cooked tongue (any kind)
8 fresh or canned long green chilis
1/2 pound mild Cheddar cheese,
   cut into 8 strips
flour
vegetable oil for frying
batter (following)

Tongue may be cooked by simmering in a court bouillon according to Step III in basic instructions, or by simmering, in lard (see burritos, page 81). If using fresh chilis, skin them by placing on a baking sheet and putting in a 450°F oven for several minutes, until chilis are well blistered but not burned. Immediately place in a brown paper bag, close tightly and allow chilis to steam in their own moisture for 10 minutes. Remove from bag, make a lengthwise slit in the chilis and remove seeds.

Wrap chili around a slice of tongue and a piece of cheese. Roll in flour. Heat oil, 1/4 inch deep, in a deep pan. Place 2 tablespoons of the batter into the pan, forming a chili shape. Place wrapped chili on top of batter and spoon an additional 2 tablespoons over top of chili. Fry until golden on underside; turn and brown other side. Repeat until all chilis and batter are used, being careful not to crowd chilis in pan. Drain on paper towels and serve with hot tomato sauce (page 133).
Serves 4

Batter

4 egg yolks, beaten until thick
4 tablespoons unbleached plain
   flour
4 egg whites, beaten stiff
pinch of salt

Gradually add flour to beaten egg yolks. Then fold in egg whites and salt. This is a good fritter batter as well. Makes enough for 8 chilis rellenos

SMOKED TONGUE WITH TOMATILLOS OR GREEN TOMATOES

1 smoked ox tongue
3 tablespoons lard
1 onion, chopped
2 cloves garlic, finely chopped
16 small new potatoes, unpeeled
4 to 5 hot green chilis, peeled,
    seeded and chopped
1-1/2 pounds tomatillos (or green
    tomatoes), cut in small wedges
2 tablespoons chopped fresh coriander
salt and freshly ground pepper

Prepare tongue according to Steps I and III in basic instructions, simmering in court bouillon. Cool in cooking liquid; remove tongue, skin and slice; reserve liquid. Line an ovenproof casserole with sliced tongue. Heat lard and sauté onion and garlic until transparent. Add potatoes, chilis, tomatillos and coriander and cook and stir for 5 minutes over medium heat. Add mixture to casserole along with enough reserved stock just to cover the tongue and potatoes. Season with salt and pepper. Cover casserole and bake in a 350°F oven for 20 to 25 minutes, or until tomatillos have practically disintegrated.
Serves 6 to 8

GRILLED TONGUE WITH ANCHOVY BUTTER

1 ox tongue, about 2 to 3 pounds
1 teaspoon anchovy paste
4 tablespoons butter, softened
2 tablespoons French bread crumbs
2 slices raw bacon, chopped

Prepare tongue according to Steps I and III in basic instructions; slice 1/2 inch thick. Combine anchovy paste and butter; spread on each slice of tongue and place in a buttered shallow baking dish. Sprinkle bread crumbs and bacon over all; place under grill until bacon is crisp and bread crumbs are slightly browned, about 10 minutes. Serve with baked potatoes.
Serves 4 to 6

CALF TONGUES WITH VEGETABLES

4 calf tongues
2 tablespoons each vegetable oil
    and butter
2 onions, sliced
4 carrots, sliced
1/4 pound mushrooms, sliced
1/2 pint beef stock
1/4 pint sour cream
2 tablespoons flour
1 teaspoon salt
1/4 teaspoon coarsely ground pepper
1/4 teaspoon nutmeg
1 tablespoon chopped parsley
4 tablespoons chopped sweet pickles

Prepare tongue according to Steps I and II in basic instructions, parboiling just 15 minutes. Skin and cut into 1/4-inch slices. Heat oil and butter in flameproof casserole and sauté tongue until lightly browned. Add vegetables and stock; cover casserole and place in a 325°F oven for 1 hour, or until tongues are tender. Heat remaining ingredients in a saucepan and bring almost to a boil. Slowly stir into tongue mixture; return to oven and continue cooking for another 15 minutes. Serve with freshly boiled potatoes of dark rye bread.
Serves 4

TONGUE

STUFFED TONGUE

1 ox tongue, about 3 to 4 pounds
6 to 8 tablespoons lemon juice
1/2 pound minced veal
1/2 pound pork sausage meat
2 ounces ham, finely chopped
2 hard-boiled eggs, chopped
2 eggs, beaten
1-1/2 teaspoons salt
1/2 teaspoon freshly ground pepper
2 tablespoons chopped fresh
    coriander or parsley
1 teaspoon crushed oregano
1 bay leaf
1 onion, quartered
6 peppercorns
1/2 pint white wine

Clean tongue and dry with paper towels. Make a deep lengthwise slit on the underside of the tongue almost to the tip. Then make several lengthwise slashes in the flesh of the meat. (This gives a nice design in cross section slices.) Then rub lemon juice into meat and let stand 10 minutes.

In the meantime, make a forcemeat by combining the veal, sausage meat, ham, hard-boiled eggs, beaten eggs, 1/2 teaspoon salt, pepper and coriander. Pile forcemeat onto flesh of tongue. Now enclose mixture in tongue by pulling cut sides of tongue together and sewing with trussing needle that has been threaded with strong thread. Don't be afraid to pull skin slightly as it is quite elastic. The forcemeat must be securely fastened.

Place stuffed tongue in large pot; add oregano, bay leaf, onion, peppercorns, 1 teaspoon salt, wine and water to cover, about 2-1/2 pints,; Cover and simmer 2 hours. Remove tongue, reserving liquid. Let tongue stand for 10 minutes before skinning and slicing. Serve with hot tomato sauce (page 133). This dish is also delicious served cold.

Serves 6 to 8

Note: Make a delicious soup for the next day by straining the reserved stock and adding 1 pound tomatoes, peeled and diced, and 6 to 8 table-**spoons** raw rice. Simmer 30 to 40 minutes or until rice is cooked.

BRAISED TONGUE
WITH OYSTER SAUCE

1 ox tongue, about 2 pounds
1 slice fresh ginger root
4 whole star anise*
1 teaspoon fennel seeds
1 tablespoon salt
2 tablespoons peanut oil
1 to 2 cloves garlic, finely chopped
4 tablespoons oyster sauce*
4 tablespoons dry sherry
1 tablespoon sugar
1/4 teaspoon Chinese 5-spice powder*
1/2 pint reserved stock
1/4 pound bamboo shoots or
    water chestnuts, sliced
1 tablespoon cornflour, mixed with
4 tablespoons cold reserved stock
fresh coriander and chopped spring
    onions for garnish

Prepare tongue according to Step I in basic instructions. Cover with fresh cold water and add ginger root, star anise, fennel seeds and salt. Bring to a boil, cover and simmer about 1 hour, or until meat is tender. Remove from pot, discard skin, cut in half lengthwise and then into 1/4-inch slices. Reserve stock.

Heat oil in a large wide pan or wok. When it sizzles, add garlic and brown lightly. Then add, while stir-frying, tongue slices, oyster sauce, sherry, sugar, 5-spice powder and reserved stock. Cover and simmer over low heat 15 minutes. Add bamboo shoots and continue cooking another 5 minutes, Thicken juices with cornflour mixture, stirring slowly into pan. Garnish with coriander and onions and serve with steamed rice.
Serves 6 to 8
*Available in Oriental stores

POZOLE

Originally made from the pig's head, this popular Mexican and Southwestern pork stew can vary according to the cook's taste. It is often served after a night of merriment.

1 pork or veal tongue
1 pound pork loin, cut in pieces
1 stewing chicken, disjointed
3 pig's feet, split lengthwise
2 onions, chopped
4 to 6 cloves garlic
2 or more tablespoons compound
    chili powder
1 pound chick peas, soaked overnight
    well rinsed
salt

Prepare tongue according to Step I in basic instructions. Clean pig's feet according to Step I in basic instructions, page 93. Cook tongue, pork loin, chicken, pig's feet, onions and garlic with 5 pints water for 1 hour, covered. Add chili powder and chick peas, and continue cooking until all meats are tender, about 1 to 1-1/2 hours longer. Remove tongue, skin and cut in pieces. Return to pot and salt to taste. Serve in soup plates with hot tortillas (page 134) and bowls of lime wedges, sliced radishes, chopped mild onions, shredded lettuce and cold tomato sauce (page 133). Each person adds condiments according to his own taste.
Serves 6 to 8

HEART

The heart may be singled out as the most neglected offal of all, mostly because of the prejudices that have long been associated with it. Up until about the first century B.C., heart, and for that matter, all offal, was eaten by hunters and warriors. It was a custom to reserve the heart, liver and kidneys for the chief or young warriors as these organs were thought to build strength and courage.

Then superstitions about food began to alter men's attitudes. So much so, that by classical Greek and Roman times, some innards were actually proscribed. In the 15th century, heart, in particular, was still in disfavor among diners. The Italians of that day considered the heart the reserve of melancholy and feared that eating it would interfere with their dedication to cultural pursuits, religious pilgrimages and enjoyment of life.

In another part of the world, in the Aztec civilization of Mexico, the living human heart was thought to be the finest offering a man could make to the gods. The Aztecs believed the gods drew strength from the human heart, a thought not far removed from that of earlier, primitive man. The hearts of animals, however, were not involved in religious sacrifices.

Heart is a versatile meat, tasting a bit like tongue, with a firm, yet tender texture. Contrary to popular opinion, it is not odd tasting, nor is it strong in smell or flavor. It is found throughout the cuisines of many cultures: in slaughter day specials or prairie dishes such as son-of-a-bitch stew; in meat pies or mince; or at feasts where the entire carcass of an animal is spit roasted, as in the days of the Caliphate or at Italian and Greek Easter celebrations. The South Americans are known for their *anticuchos* (marinated pieces of heart that are threaded on skewers and barbecued), and on the continent heart is served up in a number of braised dishes.

PREPARATION OF HEART

Heart requires very little preparation. Wash it thoroughly in cold, running water, but do not soak it. Then remove any hard connective tissue and arteries with a sharp knife. Heart is as tender as kidneys and liver, and may be sautéed quickly and served pink in the center. However, if cooked beyond this point, the meat toughens. Few cooks realize this fact. Consequently, heart more often is cooked slowly, for an extended time by moist heat methods—braising, stewing or in casseroles or ragouts. For extra tenderness, heart should be sliced lengthwise first, then cut across the grain for cooking.

PICKLED HEART

Prepare heart—any kind in any amount —according to basic instructions in preparation; cut in 1-inch cubes. Parboil for 15 minutes in water to cover with 1 stick cinnamon and a little salt. Let cool in cooking liquid; drain well. Pour vinaigrette (page 132) over heart. Place in jars with tight-fitting lids. Refrigerate. May be stored up to 1 week in the refrigerator. Eat as hors d'oeuvre or with salads. Add to cold meat plate.

GRILLED CALF HEART

After washing heart and removing arteries, pat dry and cut calf heart in half, lengthwise. Then cut in slices about 1/2 inch thick. Grill with a piece of bacon wrapped around each slice for a total of 10 minutes.

Variations: Press freshly cracked pepper into each side of heart steak. Let stand for 30 minutes or longer to absorb flavors. Wrap with bacon and grill as directed above. Or eliminate bacon and sear in a hot pan. When you turn steak over, place a pat of butter on top. Then squeeze a little lemon juice and a drop of Worcestershire sauce over the top. Remove steak and keep warm. Deglaze pan with brandy. Pour sauce over steak. Serve immediately.

STUFFED LAMB HEARTS WITH APPLES

4 lamb hearts
3 tablespoons vegetable oil
3 ounces bread crumbs
4 tablespoons melted butter
1 stalk, celery, finely chopped
1 small onion, chopped
1-1/2 teaspoons fresh sage leaves
1/4 teaspoon marjoram
salt and freshly ground pepper
4 baking apples, peeled and cored
1/2 pint dry red wine

Prepare hearts according to Step I in basic instructions. Heat oil and sear hearts well. Combine bread crumbs, butter, celery, onions, sage, marjoram, salt and pepper in a bowl. Stuff mixture into pocket of hearts and into cored apples. Place hearts in center of baking dish and surround with apples. Pour wine over all. Bake in a 350°F oven for 1-1/2 hours.
Serves 4

BAKED HEART WRAPPED IN CAUL

4 lamb, pork or veal hearts, about
    1/2 pound each
1 teaspoon Chinese 5-spice powder*
2 tablespoons each dry sherry
    and soy sauce
3 spring onions, cut in 2-inch lengths
4 sprigs fresh coriander
1/4 pound caul**

Remove arteries, veins and excess fat from hearts. Combine 5-spice powder with sherry and soy and rub well into cavity and outer sides of hearts. Divide spring onions and coriander into 4 portions and stuff into cavity of each heart. Wrap each heart securely with a piece of caul. Place seam side down in a baking dish. Bake in a 375°F oven for 1 hour. Serve with rice or barley and a watercress and orange salad.
Serves 4
Note: This may also be served as one of several dishes—Chinese family style —by slicing into bite-size pieces.
*Available in Oriental stores
**The fatty, net-like membrane investing the intestines, sometimes available on request from a good butcher.

VEAL HEARTS WITH WITH SOUR CREAM

2 pounds veal hearts (about 4)
3 tablespoons butter
1 onion, chopped
1/4 pound fresh mushrooms,
    thinly sliced
1/2 pint chicken stock
4 tablespoons Madeira
salt and freshly ground pepper
1/2 pint sour cream

Prepare hearts according to Step I in basic instructions; slice thinly. Heat 2 tablespoons butter in a flameproof casserole and sauté onion until transparent. Add remaining butter, mushrooms and hearts and sauté lightly. Add stock and Madeira; season to taste. Cover and cook in a 325°F oven 1 hour, or until hearts are tender. Stir in sour cream and cook 5 minutes longer. Serve with buttered egg noodles.
Serves 4

KOFTA

1 pound lamb heart, minced
1 pound lean lamb, minced
1 onion, very finely chopped
1 egg, beaten
1/2 teaspoon ground cinnamon or
   allspice
1/2 teaspoon ground coriander, or
1 tablespoon chopped fresh coriander
salt and freshly ground pepper

Combine all ingredients and place in refrigerator for 2 hours to allow flavors to blend. Shape into patties or sausages, and barbecue or grill, to desired doneness. To serve, pile in pocket of flat Greek pitta bread along with tomatoes, radishes, cucumbers and green peppers. Spread hot spicy sauce over all.
Serves 6 to 8
Note: Traditionally, kofta are shaped into long sausages around skewers and barbecued or grilled.

SWEET & SOUR HEART

1 ox heart, about 4 pounds
1/2 pint white wine
1/2 pint wine vinegar
2 onions, sliced
2 carrots, sliced
1 bay leaf
1 teaspoon peppercorns
2 whole cloves
4 whole allspice berries
2 tablespoons sugar
flour
3 tablespoons each butter and oil
4 to 5 ounces gingersnaps, crushed
6 to 8 tablespoons raisins

Remove arteries and excess fat from heart; leave whole and place in earthenware or china bowl. Combine wine, vinegar, 1/2 pint water, onions, carrots, bay leaf, peppercorns, cloves, allspice and sugar in a saucepan and bring almost to a boil. Pour over heart and let marinade cool, turning meat from time to time. Refrigerate at least 3 days, turning meat each day.
Remove heart from marinade and pat dry. Dust lightly with flour. Heat oil and butter in a heavy casserole. Brown meat on all sides. Add marinade to pot. Bring to a boil, reduce heat, cover and simmer for 2-1/2 hours. Remove heart to a heated platter and keep warm. Slice after 5 minutes. Strain and reserve stock.
In the meantime, make the sauce. Return 3/4 pint strained stock to pan along with gingersnaps and raisins. Cook together 5 minutes and serve with heart. Serve with potato pancakes, dumplings or parsleyed potatoes.
Serves 8

HEART

HEARTY BURGERS

1-1/2 pounds ox heart, minced
3 tablespoons chopped onion
3 tablespoons chopped green pepper
1 tablespoon chopped parsley
1 teaspoon Worcestershire sauce
1 to 1-1/2 teaspoons freshly cracked
   peppercorns

Combine heart, onions, green peppers parsley and Worcestershire. Form into 4 patties. Press cracked pepper generously into patties. Grill or barbecue over charcoal to desired doneness. Serve on hot French rolls with sliced tomatoes and avocados.
Serves 4

HEART & ASPARAGUS STIR-FRY

1 pound heart (any kind)
1 tablespoon each soy sauce and
   dry sherry
1 slice fresh ginger root, finely chopped
1 clove garlic, finely chopped
1/2 teaspoon sugar
1/2 teaspoon salt
3 tablespoons peanut oil
2 pounds asparagus, tough ends
   removed and sliced diagonally
   1/4 inch thick
1 tablespoon cornflour, mixed with
4 tablespoons water

Remove arteries and veins from heart; cut lengthwise in 1-1/2-inch strips. Then slice diagonally 1/8 inch thick. (If chicken hearts are used, leave whole.) Toss heart in soy, sherry, ginger, garlic, sugar and salt; marinate for 1 hour. Heat a wok or a wide, heavy pan, and add 2 tablespoons oil. Stir-fry heart over high heat until it begins to lose its redness. Remove to plate.
Add another tablespoon oil to wok and stir-fry asparagus for 30 seconds, stirring constantly. Add 1/4 pint water, cover and let steam rise to top. Return meat to wok, continuing to stir for 30 seconds. Thicken juices with the cornflour mixture. Serve with hot rice.
Serves 4

Variations: Broccoli, cauliflower, green beans or courgettes may be substituted for the asparagus; or toss 1 tablespoon Oriental fermented black beans (dow see), mashed, with marinade, reduce soy sauce to 1 teaspoon and omit salt; or omit soy sauce from the original recipe and add 1 tablespoon hoisin (plum) sauce and a pinch of Chinese 5-spice powder; or omit soy sauce from the original recipe and add 1 tablespoon Chinese oyster sauce. Ask for these ingredients in a Chinese store.

MONGOLIAN LAMB HEART ON SKEWERS

4 lamb hearts
2 tablespoons hoisin sauce*
1 tablespoon soy sauce
1 tablespoon dry sherry
1 tablespoon sugar
1 tablespoon peanut oil
1/4 teaspoon Chinese 5-spice powder*
1/8 or more teaspoon cayenne
1 onion, cut in 1-inch pieces
1 green pepper, cut in 1-inch pieces
toasted sesame seeds

Remove arteries and excess fat of heart; cut in 1-inch pieces. Combine hoisin, soy, sherry, sugar, oil, 5-spice powder and cayenne in a bowl and marinate heart for 2 hours, turning occasionally. Skewer heart alternately with pieces of onion and green pepper on bamboo or metal skewers. Grill over hot charcoal about 7 minutes on each side, turning frequently to prevent burning. Baste with any leftover marinade. Sprinkle with sesame seeds just before serving. Serve with steamed rice, a slice of fresh pineapple or orange slices and garnish with watercress or coriander.
Serves 4 as an entrée; 6 to 8 as an appetizer
*Available in Oriental stores

HEART À L'ORANGE

4 pork or lamb hearts
2 tablespoons each butter and
    vegetable oil
2 slices bacon, cut in 1-inch pieces
1 clove garlic, finely chopped
2 onions, chopped
2 tablespoons butter
2 tablespoons flour
3/4 pint chicken stock
1/4 pint white wine
4 tablespoons orange marmalade
6 to 8 tablespoons orange juice
2 tablespoons orange rind,
    in thin julienne strips
3 tablespoons Grand Marnier,
    Curacao or Cointreau

Prepare hearts according to Step I in basic instructions; leave whole. Heat butter and oil in a frying pan. Brown the hearts and bacon pieces. Add the garlic and onions and sauté until onions are transparent. Transfer to baking dish or casserole. Add 2 tablespoons more butter to the pan, stir in flour and gradually add stock, wine, marmalade, juice and rind. Stir constantly until smooth and thickened slightly, about 5 minutes. Add the liqueur and pour sauce over hearts. Bake in a 325°F oven for 1 hour, basting occasionally. Serve with boiled potatoes or rice pilaf and a watercress salad.
Serves 4

HEART BOURGUIGNONNE

2 pounds heart (any kind)
1/4 pound fat salt pork, parboiled
    5 minutes and cut in 1/2-inch dice
1 1/2 pint beef stock
1/2 pint red Burgundy
1 bouquet garni (page 132)
1 carrot, grated
1/2 teaspoon coarsely ground pepper
2 tablespoons butter
1/4 pound button onions
1/2 pound mushroom caps
2 carrots, cut in chunks
5 ounces fresh peas
4 tablespoons chopped parsley for garnish

Remove arteries and excess fat from heart. Heat salt pork in a flameproof casserole. Stir occasionally and sauté lightly until fat runs (about 2 tablespoons). Remove pork bits with a slotted spoon. Add the diced heart and sauté until golden on all sides. Add reserved salt pork, stock, Burgundy, bouquet garni, grated carrot and pepper. Bring just to a boil, reduce heat and simmer, uncovered, for 1-1/2 hours. Melt butter in a frying pan and sauté onions, mushrooms and carrot chunks for 5 minutes. Add to the pot; continue cooking for 20 minutes longer. During last 5 minutes of cooking period, add the peas. Remove bouquet garni and garnish casserole with parsley. Serve with buttered noodles or rice, a green salad, French bread and a good Burgundy. Fruit and cheese will complete the menu.
Serves 6 to 8

LIVER

For the most of man's history, liver has ranked above other offal as one of the most prized culinary delights. Its heritage is illustrious — whether savored by young warriors after a kill, or mixed with truffles and Cognac for fine *pâtés de foie gras.* In the *Li-Chi*, a book of ritual during China's Han Dynasty (202 B.C. to A.D. 220), liver was listed as one of the Eight Delicacies. The liver of a dog (then a common-place food of China) was wrapped in a thin casing of its own fat, roasted, then seared at the last minute to give it a crisp finishing texture. Soothsayers of ancient Greece made prophecies by consulting the shape and condition of a sacrificial animal's liver. The Roman gourmet, Apicius, claimed that the liver of a pig increased greatly in size if the animal was force-fed ripe figs and surfeited with honey and wine. And, according to Pliny, Romans coveted geese solely for their livers. Earlier, geese had been declared sacred animals because they had signaled warning when the Capitol was attacked. However, once this edict was withdrawn, geese were fattened for food.

From recordings of Marco Polo's adventures to the Far East we find that people in the mountains of Yunnan, bordering the valley of Szechwan, ate the livers of sheep, buffalo and poultry. The liver was chopped in a garlic-pepper sauce and eaten raw. Perhaps this was a forerunner of steak tartare.

In medieval times, cooked foods were sold at marketplaces, forcemeats of liver being among them. Forcemeat balls and timbales (forcemeat cooked in individual moulds or cups) soon began appearing with regularity at banquets.

Parisian menus, by the 14th century, included first courses such as cod liver-filled pastries; Platina describes a 15th-century Italian dish made from heads, feet and entrails (liver and lung) of capons and hens that was mixed with aromatic herbs and spices and bathed in vinegar; and *The Compleat Housewife*, 1727, lists many hot hors d'oeuvre consisting of liver and kidneys as well as other offal.

The French, however, truly began to understand the value of goose liver in the late 18th century. According to the epicure, Alexandre Dumas, the Alsatians blinded geese, nailed their feet to the floor and stuffed them with food until their livers swelled to 10 to 12 times normal size. These large livers were then blended into one of the greatest delicacies known to man, *pâté de foie gras*. Antonin Carême, master chef and founder of *la grande cuisine* (classic French cookery), permanently seated *foie gras* in grandeur by using it with truffles in soups, filling canapés made of *pâte feuilletée* with it, layering it over meat *en croûte* and subtly and succulently blending it into mousses.

To this day, practically every cuisine has a liver speciality – the Jewish chopped chicken liver, the Greek *kokoretsi* (lamb intestines wrapped around skewered liver and other meats) or the Finnish *maksalaati aako* (a liver pudding served for breakfast or supper).

PREPARATION OF LIVER

Liver requires a minimum of preparation whether you are dealing with chicken livers or calf, pork or lamb liver. Usually the butcher has already removed the thin membrane that encases the liver before placing it on the counter. However, if this has not been done, simply loosen the membrane by using a sharp pointed knife. Liver should never be soaked in water prior to cooking.

If liver is to be braised or roasted in 1 piece, remove the membrane and wipe with a damp cloth. If liver is to be baked or grilled in 1 piece, either lard with pork fat in 3 or 4 places, place strips of bacon over the top or rub with vegetable oil to prevent drying out. Liver contains little fat and therefore needs constant moisture. Basting will produce the same results.

Liver should be cooked over medium heat for a short period. In frying, grilling or sautéing, when the juices run clear, it is done. Liver is at its best if still pink in the center.

LIVER DUMPLINGS

1/4 pound liver (any kind), finely chopped
1 tablespoon butter
1 tablespoon finely chopped parsley
1 tablespoon finely chopped spring onions
1/2 teaspoon salt
1/4 teaspoon freshly ground pepper
1/4 teaspoon freshly grated nutmeg
1 egg, beaten
5 to 8 tablespoons bread crumbs

Combine all ingredients, adding just enough bread crumbs for mixture to hold its shape. Poach dumplings in salted water for 10 to 15 minutes; drain and cool. Then fry until golden in deep hot oil. Serve with sauerkraut or cabbage for an entrée or on toothpicks for an appetizer. Serve with Pommerol or Dijon-style mustard.
Makes 2 dozen 1-inch dumplings

Variation: Drop dumplings into 3 pints simmering rich homemade chicken stock to which diced carrot and celeriac have been added. Cook for about 15 minutes and serve dumplings with the soup.

CHICKEN LIVER ROLL-UPS

5 chicken livers, cut in half
1 large aubergine, unpeeled
salt
2 tablespoons butter
1 clove garlic, finely chopped
1 onion, thinly sliced
2 tablespoons olive oil
salt and freshly ground pepper
vegetable oil for deep-frying
hot tomato sauce (page 133)

Cut aubergine in 10 slices, sprinkle with salt and set aside for 10 minutes. Then squeeze out liquid and pat dry. Heat butter with garlic and sauté onions until transparent; add oil and the livers and sauté quickly. Season to taste with salt and pepper. Place a piece of liver on each aubergine slice, roll up and fasten with a toothpick. Fry in deep hot oil until golden. Serve as a first course with fresh tomato sauce. Also makes a nice supper dish served with a rice pilaf garnished with toasted slivered almonds.
Serves 8 as a first course; 4 to 6 as a main dish

CHOPPED LIVER

What Jewish household is unfamiliar with this dish? If you want to prepare it in the traditional kosher style, first rinse liver well in cold water, drain and sprinkle coarse salt over its entire surface. Grill to draw out blood. Wash carefully and proceed with following recipe. (This preparation applies only to ox or calf liver.)

1 pound chicken, ox or calf liver
2 tablespoons rendered chicken fat
    or margarine
1 large onion, chopped
2 to 4 hard-boiled eggs, chopped
salt and freshly ground pepper
dash of cayenne (optional)
chicken stock as needed

Sauté onions in chicken fat until transparent, add liver and brown on all sides. Remove liver and chop finely. Add eggs and season with salt and pepper to taste. If too dry, add a little chicken stock.

Variations: Follow the preceding recipe, substituting unsalted butter for the chicken fat and add the following ingredients: 2 tablespoons chopped chives and 2 tablespoons chopped parsley; or 6 tablespoons chopped shallots which have been sautéed in 1 tablespoon butter; or 1 teaspoon chopped fresh tarragon; or 1 teaspoon anchovy paste; or brandy or dry sherry instead of the chicken stock.

RUMAKI APPETIZERS

8 chicken livers, cut in thirds
24 whole water chestnuts
12 slices bacon, cut in half
4 tablespoons soy sauce
1/2 teaspoon curry powder
1/2 teaspoon freshly grated ginger root

Combine a piece of chicken liver with a water chestnut and wrap a piece of bacon around it; fasten with a toothpick. Repeat, using all livers, water chestnuts and bacon. Combine soy sauce, curry powder and ginger in a bowl. Marinate rumakis in this mixture for 1 hour. Drain, and grill, fry or deep-fry, turning frequently, until bacon is crisp.
Makes 24 rumakis

LIVER KNISHES

Filling:
1/2 pound cooked meat or poultry
   (use leftovers)
1/2 pound boiled or grilled calf liver,
   cooked just until tender
1 onion, chopped
1 stalk celery, chopped
1 green pepper, chopped
2 tablespoons rendered chicken fat
1 teaspoon salt
1/4 teaspoon freshly ground pepper

Dough:
2 pounds potatoes
3 eggs, beaten
5 tablespoons rendered chicken fat
1 teaspoon salt
8 to 10 ounces plain flour
3 tablespoons rendered chicken fat
   (for baking)

To make filling, lightly sauté onion, celery and green pepper in fat. Put through meat mincer together with the meat and livers. Season to taste. Set aside.

To make dough, boil potatoes, peel and mash well; add eggs, fat and salt; mix well. Put half the flour in the corner of a pastry board; spoon potato mixture over flour, allowing it to absorb enough flour to make it workable. Dust board with remaining flour. Flatten dough, making a 4x8-inch rectangle; spread filling down center of it; fold in half lengthwise and pinch edges together. Pat out carefully with floured fingers from center, doubling length. Cut in 1-inch pieces. Heat 3 tablespoons chicken fat in baking dish, fill with knishes and bake in a 400°F oven for 30 minutes. Turn knishes and return to oven for another 10 to 15 minutes until knishes are golden brown. Serve as appetizer or side dish. Makes 16 knishes

MATZO LIVER PANCAKES

1/4 pound finely chopped cooked
   chicken or calf liver
2 eggs, separated
1 tablespoon castor sugar
1 teaspoon salt
8 tablespoons matzo meal
6 to 8 tablespoons chicken stock
1/2 teaspoon curry powder (optional)
1 small onion, finely chopped

Beat egg whites, gradually adding sugar and salt. Lightly beat yolks and fold egg whites into them. Then gently stir in liver and all other ingredients. Use 2 to 3 tablespoons batter for each pancake. Fry on a hot greased griddle. Serve with apple sauce.
Makes 8 pancakes

LIVER PUDDING

This is a Scandinavian preparation for liver. Most often it is sliced and served for breakfast or brunch.

3/4 pound liver, finely chopped (any kind)
1 onion, finely chopped
2 tablespoons butter
3/4 pound cooked rice
6 to 8 tablespoons raisins
3 eggs, beaten
1/4 teaspoon marjoram
1 teaspoon salt
4 tablespoons honey or golden syrup
3/4 pint milk
lingonberry preserve or cranberry jelly

In a frying pan, sauté onion in butter until transparent; remove from heat and add rice. Add liver and raisins. Then combine with remaining ingredients, except preserve or jelly, and stir well. Pour batter into a buttered casserole. Dot with butter. Bake, uncovered, in a 350°F oven for 40 to 45 minutes. Serve with lingonberry preserve or cranberry jelly.
Serves 8

CALF LIVER BABAS

This is a rather spectacular way of presenting liver to your luncheon guests. It also makes a lovely first course.

1/2 pound calf liver, minced
1 tablespoon butter
1 tablespoon flour
generous 1/4 pint milk
1/2 teaspoon salt
1/4 teaspoon white pepper
1/8 teaspoon freshly grated nutmeg
dash of marjoram
1 whole egg, slightly beaten
1 egg yolk
Béarnaise sauce (page 133)

Melt butter in saucepan and blend in flour to make a paste. Slowly add milk over low heat and stir until thickened. Add seasonings. Remove from heat and blend in egg and egg yolk. Add liver, mix well and press through a fine sieve or purée in blender until smooth. Fill small buttered baba tins two-thirds full. Bake in a pan of hot water in a 350°F oven until set, about 15 to 25 minutes, depending on size of tins. Turn out and serve with Béarnaise sauce.
Makes 6 to 8, depending on size

TOMATOES STUFFED WITH LIVER

8 large firm tomatoes
1/2 pound liver (any kind)
6 to 8 tablespoons soft bread crumbs
2 tablespoons chopped spring onions
2 tablespoons milk
salt and freshly ground pepper to taste
2 eggs, beaten
2 tablespoons butter
1/4 pint sour cream

Select tomatoes of equal size. Cut slice from top and hollow out tomatoes, reserving pulp. Chop liver very fine and combine with bread crumbs, onions, milk, salt and pepper. Add eggs and mix well. Sauté the chopped liver mixture in butter for about 10 minutes, then stuff into tomatoes and cover with lids. Bake in a 350°F oven for 35 minutes. Spoon sour cream over tomatoes and bake an additional 5 minutes.
Serves 4

Variation: This same mixture may be stuffed into large flat mushrooms (omit sour cream), green peppers, cabbage leaves or pastry.

LIVER SAUTÉ

This recipe may be adapted to many varieties of liver, from calf or ox liver to pork, lamb or even game liver.

1-1/2 pounds liver, membranes
    removed and sliced 1/2 inch thick
flour
3 tablespoons butter
3 tablespoons vegetable oil
salt and freshly ground pepper

Lightly dust liver slices with flour. Heat butter and oil in a frying pan and quickly brown the liver on both sides. Do not crowd in pan; do not overcook. Transfer liver to heated platter. Salt and pepper to taste. Serve with lemon wedges if desired.
Serves 4

For liver and bacon: Place 1/2 pound bacon slices in the pan and cook until crisp; drain on paper towels. Sauté liver slices in 6 tablespoons bacon fat, following directions above. Transfer to heated platter. Garnish with bacon and chopped parsley.

For liver and onions: Prepare liver as for liver sauté. Transfer to heated platter. Have ready 2 onions, thinly sliced. Add another tablespoon of butter and oil to the pan and sauté onions until golden. Then add 1/2 teaspoon Worcestershire sauce, 1/4 teaspoon Tabasco sauce and 4 tablespoons dry red wine. Bring to a rapid boil, adjust seasonings and pour over liver.

For liver and mushrooms: Prepare liver as for liver sauté. Transfer to heated platter. Have ready 1/2 pound sliced mushrooms. Add 3 more tablespoons butter to the pan and sauté mushrooms over medium heat for 5 minutes. Then add 1/2 teaspoon tarragon, 1 teaspoon chives and 4 tablespoons dry white wine. Bring to a rapid boil, adjust seasonings and immediately pour over liver.

SAUTÉED LIVER WITH APPLE FRITTERS

4 slices liver (about 1-1/2 pounds)
8 1/2-inch onion rings
8 apple rings
beer batter (following)
oil for deep-frying

Prepare liver as for liver sauté (preceding). Transfer to heated platter. In the meantime, prepare beer batter. Then dip onion and apple rings into batter and fry in deep hot oil until golden. Pile on top of liver and serve.
Serves 4

BEER BATTER

1/2 pint light beer
2 eggs, beaten
4 ounces plain flour, sifted with pinch
    of salt

Beat beer into eggs. Then gradually add flour and salt, beating all the while. Use for apple and onion rings.

Sautéed chicken livers are a favorite breakfast specialty in many countries. The Mexicans serve theirs with tortillas and maybe some cinnamon-flavored orange slices. The Germans might make up potato pancakes to go along with theirs. Use your imagination. The following are two recipes for breakfast sautés.

MEXICAN CHICKEN LIVERS

1 pound chicken livers
flour seasoned with salt and pepper
6 to 8 tablespoons chopped spring
  onions
1/2 pound mushrooms, sliced
4 tablespoons butter
4 tablespoons Madeira or sherry

Dust livers with seasoned flour. Sauté onions and mushrooms in butter until lightly browned. Add livers and sauté for 10 minutes. Add Madeira and simmer for 5 minutes to allow flavors to blend. Serve with hot tomato sauce (page 133).
Serves 4

CHICKEN LIVER SAUTÉ, HUNGARIAN STYLE

1 pound chicken livers, halved,
  and dusted with
1 tablespoon flour
2 onions, sliced
3 tablespoons vegetable oil
  or butter
1 tablespoon paprika, or to taste
  seeded and chopped
3 large tomatoes, peeled and chopped
salt and freshly ground pepper to taste

Sauté onions in 2 tablespoons of the oil until transparent. Add livers and sauté about 5 minutes; remove to side. Add remaining oil to pan; add paprika and tomatoes and cook over medium heat for 10 minutes. Adjust seasonings with salt and pepper. Add chicken livers and onions that were set aside; continue cooking another 10 minutes. Good served over an omelette.
Serves 4

BASQUE CHICKEN LIVER SAUTÉ

1 pound chicken livers, dusted with
1 tablespoon flour
2 tablespoons olive oil
1 clove garlic, finely chopped
2 tablespoons butter
2 ounces button mushrooms, sliced
6 to 8 tablespoons dry white wine
1 tablespoon chopped parsley
salt and freshly ground pepper

Heat oil with garlic and sauté livers until browned. Add butter and mushrooms and sauté quickly. Add wine, parsley and seasonings. Cover and simmer for 3 minutes. Serve with saffron rice or wild rice.
Serves 4

CRISP-FRIED CHICKEN LIVERS

1 pound chicken livers, cut in half
1 tablespoon soy sauce
1 tablespoon dry sherry
1 teaspoon very finely chopped
    fresh ginger root
1 clove garlic, finely chopped
2 tablespoons finely chopped spring
    onions
8 tablespoons plain flour
2 tablespoons cornflour
peanut oil for deep-frying

Marinate chicken livers in mixture of
soy sauce, sherry, ginger, garlic and
spring onions for 1 hour. Then add
flour and cornflour, mixing only to
blend. Drop the chicken livers, one at
a time, in deep, hot oil and fry for 3 to
5 minutes until brown, crispy and
cooked through but not dry. These
make wonderful appetizers served with
hot mustard, ketchup or soy.
Serves 4

Variation: Gizzards and hearts may be
prepared as above. Cut gizzards in half
to separate 2 sections; score in criss-
cross manner to allow for even cooking. Gizzards require 1 or 2 minutes
longer cooking time than livers or
hearts.

CURRIED LIVER

1-1/2 pounds lamb, calf or chicken
    livers
2 onions, thinly sliced
2 cloves garlic, finely chopped
2 tablespoons each butter and
    vegetable oil
1 or more dried red chilis, finely
    chopped
1/2 teaspoon freshly grated ginger root
1 tablespoon finely chopped coriander
1/4 teaspoon cumin
1/2 teaspoon turmeric
1/2 teaspoon coarsely ground black
    pepper
1 teaspoon salt
1/2 pint coconut milk*

Remove membranes from liver and cut
in 1-inch pieces. (If using chicken
livers, cut them in half.) Sauté onions
and garlic in butter and oil until transparent. Add chili, spices and seasonings; continue sautéing for 2 minutes
longer. Add liver and sauté 3 more
minutes. Stir in coconut milk; simmer,
uncovered, for 8 to 10 minutes, or just
until liver is cooked. Serve over plain
rice or a saffron-flavored rice with condiments such as chutney, sieved egg

*Bring 1 cup unsweetened grated coco-
nut and 1 cup milk to a boil. Cool and
strain through a fine sieve.

yolk and chopped egg whites (prepared separately by tradition), toasted
coconut, chopped peanuts, chopped
spring onions, cucumbers and raisins.
Serves 4 to 6

SWEET & SOUR CHICKEN LIVERS WITH PINEAPPLE

1 pound chicken livers
1/2 pint pineapple juice (or part
    water)
2 tablespoons vinegar
2 tablespoons sugar
2 tablespoons ketchup
2 tablespoons cornflour
1/4 pound pineapple chunks
1 green pepper, cut in 1-inch chunks
1 spanish onion, cut in 1-inch chunks
1 tablespoon toasted sesame seeds

Prepare livers in same manner as preceding recipe for crisp-fried chicken
livers; keep warm. To make sauce, mix
together pineapple juice, vinegar,
sugar, ketchup and cornflour. Cook
over medium heat, stirring constantly,
until mixture comes almost to the boil
and is slightly thickened. Add pineapple, green pepper and onion; again
bring just to the boil. Pour over
chicken livers and sprinkle with
toasted sesame seeds. Serve with rice.
Serves 4

STUFFED POUSSINS WITH CHICKEN LIVERS

4 poussins (about 1 pound each)
3/4 pound chicken livers, cut in half
1/4 pound button mushrooms, chopped
4 tablespoons ham, cut in thin strips
4 tablespoons pistachios or pine nuts
2 tablespoons butter
salt and freshly ground pepper
juice of 1/2 lemon
bacon strips

Sauté chicken livers, mushrooms, ham and nuts in butter. Stuff mixture loosely into birds. Truss with white string or skewers. Rub birds with salt, pepper and lemon juice. Place a couple strips of bacon over the birds and roast 45 minutes to 1 hour in a 350°F oven.
Serves 4

CHICKEN LIVERS & SPAGHETTI

1 pound chicken livers, quartered
flour seasoned with salt and pepper
1 clove garlic, finely chopped
2 onions, chopped
4 tablespoons olive oil
1 pint thick fresh tomato purée
1 6-ounce can tomato paste
1 tablespoon chopped fresh basil
1 sprig rosemary
1/2 teaspoon crushed oregano
1/4 teaspoon cinnamon
salt and cayenne to taste
6 to 8 tablespoons dry red wine
1/2 pound spaghetti or green noodles
freshly grated Parmesan cheese

Sauté garlic and onions in 2 tablespoons of the olive oil. Add tomatoes, tomato paste, seasonings and wine. Simmer for about 1 hour, stirring from time to time, until smooth and slightly thickened.

Lightly dust chicken livers with seasoned flour and sauté in remaining 2 tablespoons oil. Add to sauce and cook for 10 minutes.

In the meantime, cook spaghetti or noodles al dente; drain and put on heated platter. Pour chicken liver sauce over all and serve with freshly grated Parmesan cheese, crusty bread and a green salad.
Serves 4 to 6

TUSCAN MIXED GRILL

6 small slices pork loin
6 small pieces boned chicken
6 slices pork liver
6 small rib lamb chops
12 slices lean bacon, halved
24 leaves fresh sage
2 sprigs rosemary, ground in a mortar
freshly ground pepper
6 to 8 tablespoons olive oil
3 to 4 juniper berries, crushed, or
1/2 teaspoon fennel seeds, bruised
salt to taste

Skewer pork, chicken, liver and lamb, placing a bacon strip and sage leaf between each. Sprinkle with rosemary and freshly ground pepper to taste. Place skewers, side by side in a shallow baking dish and pour olive oil over them. Add the juniper berries and marinate 3 to 4 hours. Grill over charcoal, turning frequently, about 15 minutes, or until meats are cooked but still juicy. Sprinkle with salt. Or, place on a rack in a roasting tin and roast in a 450°F oven for about the same time. Serve with a rice pilaf tossed with raisins which have first been plumped up in hot water.

Serves 6

SOUR PORK LIVER

1 pound pork liver, membranes
  removed, cut in strips
1 onion, chopped
4 slices bacon, diced
1 tablespoon flour
1/4 pint chicken stock
4 tablespoons lemon juice
salt and freshly ground pepper to taste

Fry onion and bacon together for 5 minutes. Then add liver and sauté another 2 minutes over high heat. Transfer to heated platter. Add flour to pan and stir well. Gradually add stock and bring to boil, cooking for 5 minutes. Add lemon juice; adjust seasonings. Pour sauce over liver. Serve immediately.
Serves 4

LIVER PAPRIKA

1-1/2 pounds calf or lamb liver,
  cut in 1-inch cubes
3 tablespoons flour
1 tablespoon paprika
1/2 teaspoon salt
1/2 teaspoon freshly ground pepper
4 tablespoons olive oil
1 onion, thinly sliced
4 tablespoons chopped parsley
1/2 pint sour cream

Remove membranes from liver. Then combine flour with paprika, salt and pepper and sprinkle on liver. Heat 3 tablespoons of the oil in a frying pan. Sauté liver cubes until brown, about 3 to 5 minutes. Transfer to heated platter. Add another tablespoon oil to the pan and sauté onion slices and parsley until onions are transparent. Add sour cream and heat without boiling so as not to curdle sour cream. Pour over liver and serve immediately. Serve with buttered noodles or boiled potatoes. Serves 4

Variation: Chicken livers, halved, may be substituted in this recipe.

LIVER & VEGETABLE STIR-FRY

1 pound liver (any kind)
1 tablespoon hoisin sauce* or
    soy sauce
2 tablespoons dry sherry
1 teaspoon sugar
1/2 teaspoon fried sesame oil**
2 stalks celery, cut in 1/4-inch
    diagonal slices
1/4 pound bamboo shoots, sliced
1/2 pound mangetout peas
1/4 pound button mushrooms,
    left whole
salt to taste
1/4 pint chicken stock
1 tablespoon cornflour
peanut oil for stir-frying

Cut liver in 1/4x1-inch-thick slices, or cut chicken livers into thirds. Combine hoisin, sherry, sugar and sesame oil in a bowl and marinate liver for 30 minutes. Heat 2 tablespoons oil in a wok (or use a wide, deep heavy frying pan). Add celery, bamboo shoots, mangetout peas and mushrooms; salt lightly and stir-fry for 2 minutes. Add stock, cover and let steam rise to top (about 1 minute). Do not overcook. Remove vegetables to heated dish; keep warm. Quickly return wok to heat and add 3 tablespoons oil. Sprinkle livers with cornflour and stir lightly. Add livers to very hot wok and stir-fry about 1-1/2 minutes to brown. Place on top of vegetables and serve immediately with hot rice.
Serves 4
 *Available in Oriental stores.
**The dark seasoning oil available in Oriental markets.

BAKED CALF LIVER

about 1-1/2 pounds calf liver in one
    piece
1/4 pint wine vinegar
vegetable oil
1 onion, sliced
4 sprigs parsley
1 sprig thyme
salt and freshly ground pepper to taste
4 slices bacon

Brush liver with oil. Combine vinegar, onion, parsley, thyme, salt and pepper and marinate liver for 24 hours in the refrigerator. Remove from refrigerator and let stand 1 hour before roasting. Place in a roasting tin and top with bacon, then onion slices from marinade. Bake in a 375°F oven for 25 to 30 minutes, basting from time to time.
Serves 6

STUFFED CALF LIVER

1 2-pound piece calf liver
1/4 pound bacon, diced
1 onion, chopped
8 tablespoons bread crumbs
2 tablespoons finely chopped parsley
1 egg, beaten
1/4 pint sour cream
salt and freshly ground pepper to taste
4 tablespoons vegetable oil

Make a slash through center of liver to form pocket. Put bacon, onion, bread-crumbs and parsley in a frying pan. Fry until onions are transparent; cool. Combine bacon mixture with egg and sour cream and season with salt and pepper. Put mixture into liver pocket and truss with white string or skewers. Place in a shallow baking dish and rub well with oil. Bake in a 350°F oven for about 1 hour. Slice liver and pour any pan juices over it. Serve with brown rice or dumplings.
Serves 6 to 8

KIDNEYS

Possibly, when men of Paleolithic times killed their prey and carved up the flesh for transport home, they rewarded themselves with a banquet of the more perishable parts — kidneys, liver, brains, heart, the fat behind the eyeballs and the soft internal organs. Kidneys have certainly played an important role in man's diet. Generally regarded as one of the most nourishing of all foods, kidneys have been eaten by the peoples of practically every culture, and especially by the Chinese (pork), Middle Easterners (lamb), Spanish (veal) and English (veal and ox).

Animal kidneys have been found among the relics evacuated from Egyptian tombs of the 12th century B.C. Though the Egyptian peasant diet consisted mainly of beer, bread and lentils, the rich feasted upon the kidneys and flesh of antelopes and gazelles. In later times, in the courts of the caliphs about the 10th century A.D., kidneys of kid were strung beside the carcass of the animal, delicately flavored with mint and lemon juice and roasted over an open fire. Kidneys were popular at medieval banquets, being included in such dishes as meat pies and pasties. This might have been a forerunner to the traditional British steak and kidney pie.

Kidneys did pass through a period of rejection during the Italian Renaissance. The people generally believed they were responsible for man's bad humors. (The heart, liver and spleen were also condemned.) However, their unpopularity was short-lived, as the chefs of 18th and 19th century France and England rediscovered them and used them extravagantly. Within the volume of *The Compleat Housewife,* printed in England in 1727, one can find many dishes using kidneys — everyday dishes as well as more elaborate hot hors d'oeuvre.

Kidneys are also valued because of the fat that encases them. This is suet, the finest of all fat. It makes marvelous pastry for beef or other pies and should be used exclusively in English plum pudding or mincemeat.

PREPARATION OF KIDNEYS

It is curious that kidneys have taken on different shapes within the bodies of various quadrupeds. Ox or veal kidneys are multi-lobed and elongated, while the kidneys of lamb and pork have a single lobe that is bean-shaped. Many people object to ox and pork kidneys because of their strong odor. However, if they are properly cleaned and soaked, the objectionable odor dissipates. A perfectly cooked kidney is a sign of a good chef. Keep in mind that kidneys must be grilled or sautéed quickly to be tender. Overcooking toughens them and long, slow cooking is required to make them tender again.

Step I: Cleaning

Remove outside membrane from all kidneys with a sharp, pointed knife. Split ox or pork kidneys in half lengthwise and remove white core and excess fat from center with a sharp knife; this is not necessary for lamb or veal kidneys. Any fat surrounding the kidney should be reserved for later use; this is true suet, the best of all fat.

Step II: Soaking

Beef and pork kidneys should be soaked in acidulated water (1 table-spoon lemon juice or vinegar to 3/4 pint water) or buttermilk for 1 hour. Never soak veal or lamb kidneys as they have a tendency to soak up too much water due to their more delicate flavor and texture.

Drain the kidneys and pat dry before proceeding with recipe (unless parboiling is to follow). Additionally, baking soda or salt may be rubbed into ox or pork kidneys to remove any remaining pungent odor. Rinse well.

Step III: Parboiling

Parboil pork or ox kidneys just 1 minute to remove excess blood and clinging parts. Add 1 tablespoon lemon juice to the water, if desired. Do not overcook. This is especially recommended in many of the Chinese recipes as it makes the juice clearer when stir-frying.

PORK KIDNEYS
IN WHISKY SOUP

This is a very clever way of eating your whisky. The Chinese found this out centuries ago when they first combined two "warming" ingredients— fresh ginger and strong rice wine. It's a perfect way to ward off the chill of a cold winter's evening.

1-1/2 pounds pork kidneys
2 tablespoons peanut oil
4 tablespoons thinly sliced fresh
    ginger root
1 tablespoon soy sauce
1 teaspoon salt
6 to 8 tablespoons Scotch or
    bourbon (or gin)

Prepare kidneys according to Steps I and II in basic instructions, splitting and cleaning kidneys before soaking. Then parboil in salted water (1 teaspoon salt to 1-1/2 pints water) for 1 minute; drain. Heat oil in a pot and when it just begins to smoke, add kidneys and ginger and stir-fry for a minute. Then add soy, salt and 2 tablespoons of the whisky. Brown slightly before adding remaining whisky and 2-1/2 pints water. Bring just to a boil, reduce heat and simmer for 10 minutes. Serve immediately in soup bowls. Serves 4 to 6

SOUP WITH KIDNEY DUMPLINGS

1 veal kidney
1 tablespoon butter
1 tablespoon beef marrow (scraped
    from a 3-inch marrow bone)
8 tablespoons white bread crumbs
1 tablespoon flour
1 tablespoon finely chopped parsley
salt and freshly ground pepper to taste
3 egg yolks, beaten
3 pints beef stock

Remove any fat or membrane from kidney according to Step I in basic instructions; pat dry and finely chop. Melt butter in a frying pan. Cook kidneys and marrow for 5 minutes. Put mixture into a bowl. Add bread crumbs, flour, parsley, salt and pepper. Bind all with egg yolks. Mixture should be firm (more flour might be necessary). Shape into 3/4-inch balls. Bring stock to a simmer and drop dumplings into stock. Cook 10 minutes. Serve in soup tureen or in individual bowls.
Serves 6

GRILLED KIDNEYS

Keep kidneys in large pieces if possible; lamb and veal kidneys are actually nice grilled whole. If split, skewer flat with toothpicks to keep edges from rolling up; this is not necessary if smaller pieces or cubes are used. Spread cut side of kidney with melted butter and sprinkle with fine bread crumbs. Set on grill rack, cut side up. Cook for several minutes. Turn over, brush again with melted butter, sprinkle with more bread crumbs and grill a minute or 2 longer. Serve with lemon wedges, crisp bacon and French fries or boiled potatoes. Or serve on toast or a bed of risotto or pilaf.

Variation: Blend butter with herbs such as parsley, tarragon, chives, shallots, or prepared Dijon-style mustard or lemon juice.

Variation: Skewer kidneys alternately with squares of parboiled salt pork or bacon and sautéed mushroom caps.

SKEWERED KIDNEYS

12 lamb or veal kidneys
6 to 8 tablespoons olive oil
salt and freshly ground pepper to taste
1/4 teaspoon thyme
1/4 teaspoon dry mustard
1/4 teaspoon mace
dash of cayenne

Prepare kidneys according to Step I in basic instructions. Split lengthwise and thread each piece on a wooden skewer. Place in a shallow pan, cut side up.
Make a marinade by combining remaining ingredients and pour over kidneys. Marinate 10 minutes, turning frequently. Drain. Place skewered kidneys cut side down on grill rack or barbecue grid. Grill 4 to 5 minutes on first side; turn and grill about 3 minutes longer.
Serves 4 to 6

Variation: Follow above recipe, but thread marinated kidneys on skewers along with whole mushrooms, parboiled button onions and bacon squares.

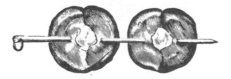

KIDNEYS IN THEIR OVERCOATS

This is a traditional Irish dish that is often served for breakfast. It would be good served with sautéed potatoes and scrambled eggs. For lunch, serve on crisp toast accompanied by boiled potatoes in their jackets and braised fresh spinach or cabbage.

Ask the butcher to leave on the outer layer of fat (the suet) that surrounds the kidneys. This fat gets wonderfully crispy in cooking, at the same time preventing overcooking and loss of juices. Allow 2 to 3 lamb kidneys (veal kidneys would be good, too) per person. Place in a shallow baking dish in a preheated 400°F oven for 30 minutes, or until fat is melted and crispy. Split open on crisp (unbuttered) toast; salt and pepper to taste.

KIDNEYS IN RED WINE

1 pound kidneys (any kind)
4 tablespoons or more butter
1 onion, chopped
1/4 pound mushrooms, sliced
1/2 teaspoon tarragon
1 tablespoon chopped parsley
6 to 8 tablespoons dry red wine
4 tablespoons beef stock
salt and freshly ground pepper to taste

Prepare kidneys according to Steps I and II (if pork or ox) in basic instructions. Drain and slice in bite-size pieces. Heat butter in frying pan. Sauté kidneys over high heat; remove and keep warm. Add onion, mushrooms, tarragon and parsley to pan, sautéing until onions are transparent. Deglaze pan with wine and stock; bring to a boil. Return kidneys to pan, season with salt and pepper and cook several minutes until very hot. Serve on dry toast or over fluffy rice.
Serves 4

VEAL KIDNEYS WITH MADEIRA & SOUR CREAM

4 veal kidneys
flour
2 tablespoons each butter and
    vegetable oil
8 tablespoons Madeira
2 tablespoons chopped chives
4 tablespoons sour cream
salt and freshly ground pepper
dash of cayenne

Prepare kidneys according to Step I in basic instructions and thinly slice. Dust with flour and sauté quickly in hot butter and oil until golden. Remove to a warm platter; keep warm. Deglaze pan with Madeira; add chives. Reduce heat and add sour cream, stirring all the while; do not boil. Season with salt, pepper and cayenne. Pour sauce over kidneys.
Serves 4

VEAL KIDNEYS IN WHITE WINE

4 veal kidneys, or
8 lamb kidneys
2 tablespoons olive oil
3 tablespoons butter
2 tablespoons chopped parsley
1 tablespoon finely chopped shallots
2 tablespoons flour
1/2 pint dry white wine
1/4 pint chicken or beef stock
1 tablespoon lemon juice
salt and freshly ground pepper to taste

Prepare kidneys according to Step I in basic instructions; cut into 1-inch slices. Heat olive oil and 2 tablespoons butter in a frying pan and sauté kidneys on both sides. Reduce heat and add parsley and shallots. Cook several minutes; remove to warm dish and keep warm. Add flour to the pan; then deglaze with wine and stock, stirring constantly, until smooth and thickened. Remove from heat and add 1 tablespoon butter, lemon juice, salt and pepper. Pour over kidneys.
Serves 4

SAUTÉED KIDNEYS ANDALUSIA

4 veal kidneys
6 tablespoons olive oil
6 to 8 tablespoons chopped ham
    (prosciutto or Westphalian ham
    preferred)
1 large onion, finely chopped
2 cloves garlic, finely chopped
1 small bay leaf
1 tablespoon flour
1/4 pint chicken stock
2 tablespoons finely chopped parsley
6 to 8 tablespoons pale dry sherry
salt and freshly ground pepper to taste

Prepare kidneys according to Step I in basic instructions. Split in half lengthwise; then cut into 1-inch slices. Heat 4 tablespoons oil in a frying pan over high heat. Add ham, onions, garlic and bay leaf. Reduce heat slightly and sauté until onions are transparent. Add flour and mix thoroughly. Add stock and cook, stirring constantly, until mixture is smooth and thickened. Add parsley; reduce heat and cook 3 minutes longer.

Heat remaining oil in another frying pan. Add kidneys and sauté quickly on both sides. Transfer kidneys to plate. Deglaze pan with sherry; bring to a boil. Return kidneys to pan along with onion sauce. Heat through; adjust seasonings with salt and pepper.
Serves 6

VEAL KIDNEYS BORDELAISE

6 veal kidneys
salt and freshly ground pepper to taste
5 tablespoons butter
4 tablespoons finely chopped shallots
1/4 pint dry red wine
2 tablespoons flour
generous 1/2 pint rich beef stock
2 tablespoons tomato paste
pinch of thyme
1 teaspoon lemon juice
2 tablespoons chopped beef marrow
1 tablespoon chopped parsley

Prepare kidneys according to Step I in basic instructions; cut into 1-inch slices. Season well with salt and pepper. Heat butter in a frying pan. Sauté kidneys quickly over high heat. Transfer to flameproof casserole. Add shallots to the pan and sauté until transparent. Add wine and reduce to 3 tablespoons over high heat. Combine flour with two-thirds of the stock and blend well. Add this mixture along with remaining stock, tomato paste, thyme, lemon juice, marrow and parsley to the pan, blending well; cook until thickened. Pour all the sauce over the kidneys and heat just until simmering.
Serves 6

VEAL KIDNEYS FLAMBÉ

6 veal kidneys
4 tablespoons butter
1 tablespoon finely chopped shallots
18 mushroom caps
2 tablespoons brandy, warmed
4 tablespoons dry sherry
2 to 3 tablespoons double cream
salt and freshly ground pepper to taste
watercress or chopped parsley
    for garnish

Remove membrane from kidneys according to Step I in basic instructions; do not wash or soak. Slice crosswise in 1/4-inch slices. Heat butter in sauté pan; add shallots and sauté until transparent. Add mushrooms and kidneys and cook until lightly browned. Pour warmed brandy over all and ignite. When flame dies down, add sherry. Simmer gently 1 or 2 minutes to reduce slightly. Stir in cream; adjust seasonings with salt and pepper. Allow sauce to thicken slightly. Garnish with watercress or parsley; serve with rice.
Serves 6

SAUTÉED PORK KIDNEYS

4 pork kidneys, about 1 pound
buttermilk
3 tablespoons bacon fat
1 onion, chopped
1 large unpeeled apple, sliced
1/2 teaspoon caraway seeds
1/2 teaspoon freshly ground pepper
1 teaspoon flour
beef stock as needed

Soak and clean kidneys according to Steps I and II in basic instructions, using buttermilk in soaking liquid. Rinse, pat dry and cut into slices. Heat fat in a large frying pan. Sauté onion until transparent. Add kidneys and brown on both sides, about 2 minutes. Add apples, caraway seeds and pepper and continue cooking over medium-high heat for about 8 minutes. Then sprinkle with flour, add a little stock and cook until slightly thickened. Serve with sauerkraut, potatoes and black bread.
Serves 4

VEAL & KIDNEY SAUTÉ

2 veal kidneys
1 pound veal cutlets, cut
    1/4 inch thick
1/2 teaspoon salt
1/4 teaspoon freshly ground pepper
4 or more tablespoons butter
4 ounces button mushrooms
4 tablespoons dry sherry
1/2 pound cooked vegetables, either
    carrot strips and green beans, or
    broad beans and button onions

Clean, pat dry and slice kidneys into bite-size pieces. Season veal with salt and pepper. Heat 3 tablespoons butter in a frying pan. Sauté veal on both sides; place on warm platter and keep warm. Add remaining butter, kidneys and mushrooms and sauté until kidneys are tender. Remove to platter and keep warm. Deglaze pan with sherry and bring to a boil; adjust seasonings and pour over meat. Garnish platter with cooked vegetables.
Serves 4

PORK KIDNEY SAUTÉ
WITH PILAF

6 pork kidneys
4 or more tablespoons butter
1 onion, chopped
4 tablespoons chopped parsley
1-1/2 cups (about 9 ounces) white or
    brown rice
2-3/4 cups beef stock, heated to
    boiling point
4 tablespoons slivered, blanched
    almonds
1 tablespoon olive oil
6 to 8 tablespoons dry white wine
salt and freshly ground pepper to taste
dash of cayenne

Prepare kidneys according to Steps I
and II in basic instructions; slice. Continue with Step III. Heat butter in a
2-1/2-pint saucepan; add onion, parsley and rice and fry until lightly
browned. Add stock, cover and simmer until liquid has evaporated and
rice is cooked through (20 to 30 minutes for white rice, 30 to 40 minutes
for brown rice).

In the meantime, sauté almonds in oil
until golden. Remove from pan; set
aside. Add a little butter if necessary
to the same pan; add kidneys and
sauté 4 to 5 minutes. Set aside and
keep warm. Deglaze pan with wine,
add seasonings and reduce to half.
Return kidneys to pan and heat
through. Pile cooked rice on serving
platter in a ring, place sautéed kidneys
in the center and garnish with
almonds.
Serves 6

VEAL SCHNITZEL
WITH KIDNEYS

2 veal kidneys
1 pound veal cutlets, pounded
    1/4 inch thick
flour for dredging
6 tablespoons butter
8 large mushroom caps
5 tablespoons beef stock
5 tablespoons dry sherry
1/4 teaspoon freshly grated nutmeg
1/4 teaspoon paprika
salt and freshly ground pepper to taste

Prepare kidneys according to Step I in
basic instructions; cut each kidney
into 8 slices. Dredge cutlets with flour.
Heat 4 tablespoons butter in a frying
pan. Add the cutlets and brown on both
sides; remove and keep warm. Add
remaining butter, kidneys and mushrooms; sauté quickly over high heat, 1
or 2 minutes. Top cutlets with kidneys
and mushrooms. Keep warm. Deglaze
pan with stock and sherry. Add nutmeg, paprika, salt and pepper. Bring to
boil and reduce by half; pour over
meat. Serve hot with boiled potatoes
and glazed carrots.
Serves 4

Variations: Follow the above recipe,
substituting 1/2 pound chicken livers
for the veal kidneys. Or follow the
above recipe, substituting boned
chicken breasts for the veal cutlets.
Either veal kidneys or 1/2 pound
chicken livers may be used with the
chicken breasts.

KIDNEY, TOMATO & GREEN PEPPER STIR-FRY

1 pound ox or pork kidneys
2 tablespoons peanut oil
2 thin slices fresh ginger root, finely chopped
1 clove garlic, finely chopped
1 tablespoon soy sauce
2 tablespoons dry sherry
1 pound tomatoes, cut in wedges
1 green pepper, cut in 1-inch pieces
1 onion, cut in 1-inch pieces
1 tablespoon sugar
1 teaspoon cornflour, blended with
4 tablespoons water
salt to taste

Soak and clean kidneys according to Steps I and II in basic instructions; cut into 1-inch pieces. Then parboil pieces in salted water (1 teaspoon salt to 1-1/2 pints water) for 1 minute only; drain. Heat oil in a large, heavy frying pan over high heat; add ginger and garlic and let sizzle 30 seconds. Add kidneys and stir-fry until lightly browned (another 30 seconds). Then add soy, sherry, tomatoes, green pepper, onion and sugar. Cover and let steam rise to top and vegetables heat through, about 3 to 5 minutes. Thicken juices with cornflour mixture, stirring constantly. Adjust seasonings. Serve immediately with steamed rice.
Serves 4 to 6

Variations: Lamb or veal kidneys may be substituted for the ox or pork kidneys in the above recipe. Omit parboiling in this case. For a spicier version, follow the above recipe, adding 1 finely chopped dried red chili when adding the vegetables. For kidney and asparagus stir-fry, follow the above recipe, omitting tomatoes and green pepper. Substitute 1-1/2 pounds asparagus, sliced on the diagonal 1/4 inch thick, and 1/4 pint water. For kidney and broccoli stir-fry, follow above recipe, omitting tomatoes and green pepper. Substitute 1-1/2 pounds broccoli, cut in flowerets and 1/4 pound thinly sliced and chopped ham. Omit salt in this case.

KIDNEYS WITH JUNIPER BERRIES

2 pounds ox or pork kidneys
salt and freshly ground pepper to taste
4 tablespoons butter
6 to 8 tablespoons dry red wine
4 juniper berries, crushed
1 teaspoon grated lemon peel

Soak and clean kidneys according to Steps I and II in basic instructions. Cut in bite-size pieces and sprinkle with salt and pepper. Heat butter and brown kidneys on both sides. Add wine and juniper berries, cover and cook 2 minutes. Uncover, reduce heat, and cook about 5 to 7 minutes longer, until kidneys are cooked through and juices are reduced by half. Stir in lemon peel at last minute. Adjust seasonings.
Serves 4 to 6

ROAST LEG OF VEAL & KIDNEYS

5-pound leg of veal, boned
2 veal kidneys, with their fat
1 tablespoon paprika
salt and freshly ground pepper to taste
4 tablespoons butter
1/2 pint chicken stock
4 tablespoons double cream or sour cream

Lay boned veal flat. Sprinkle kidneys with paprika and place in center of veal; season with salt and pepper. Roll up veal tightly around kidneys and secure with string in several places. Preheat oven to 400°. Place butter in roasting tin and allow to melt. Place roast in tin and brown for 15 minutes, turning from time to time. Add tne stock to the tin. Reduce temperature to 325°F; continue roasting, uncovered, for 2 hours, or until done, basting frequently. Remove to warm platter. Thicken pan juices with cream; serve separately. Complete menu with parsleyed potatoes or egg noodles and boiled red cabbage.
Serves 8

Variation: Sprinkle veal with chopped fresh herbs such as parsley, shallots, chervil and chives before tying roast.

KIDNEY RAGOUT

1 pound ox kidney
4 tablespoons butter
1 onion, chopped
4 tablespoons flour
3/4 pint beef stock
4 tablespoons dry red wine
4 tablespoons tomato paste
salt and freshly ground pepper to taste
1 small sprig fresh thyme, or
1/4 teaspoon dried thyme

Soak and clean kidneys according to Steps I and II in basic instructions; drain and cut in thin slices. Heat butter in frying pan. Sauté kidneys and onions until kidneys are golden and onions are transparent; remove and set aside. Stir flour into pan and cook 3 to 4 minutes, scraping edges to remove clinging particles. Add stock, wine and tomato paste and cook until thickened. Add seasonings and kidneys and heat through. Serve over fluffy rice.
Serves 4

STEAK & KIDNEY PIE

3/4 pound veal, ox or lamb kidneys
2 ounces kidney suet, finely chopped,
   or half butter and half suet
1 onion, chopped
1-1/2 pounds chuck steak,
   cut in 3/4-inch cubes
1-1/4 pints beef stock
1 teaspoon salt
1/2 teaspoon freshly ground pepper
1 tablespoon Worcestershire sauce
3 tablespoons flour
1/2 recipe puff pastry (page 134)

Prepare kidneys according to Steps I and II in basic instructions, depending on variety of kidneys used. Cut into 1/2-inch cubes and set aside. Heat suet in a large, heavy pan until melted; add onion and sauté until transparent. Then add steak and brown; add stock, salt, pepper and Worcestershire sauce, cover, and simmer for 1-1/2 hours, or until meat is tender. Add kidneys. Thicken juices by sifting flour gradually into the pan, stirring all the while. Remove from heat and let cool. Pour the contents of the pan into a 3-pint pie dish. Fit a pastry lid on top and seal edges. Make vents to allow steam to escape and decorate top with pastry trimmings if desired. Bake in a 425°F oven for 1 hour, or until crust is golden. Serves 6

Variation: Follow above recipe, adding 1 dozen oysters at the same time as the kidneys. Four ounces mushrooms, sliced and sautéed may also be added along with a splash of Madeira to the meat filling just before fitting on the pastry lid.

KIDNEY HOT POT

3 to 4 lamb kidneys
2 pounds boneless stewing lamb,
    trimmed of excess fat
2 pounds potatoes, peeled and sliced
3 onions, thinly sliced
3 carrots, sliced
salt and freshly ground pepper to taste
12 oysters (optional)
1 tablespoon cornflour
3/4 pint beef stock
4 tablespoons butter, melted

Wash and clean kidneys according to Steps I and II in basic instructions; cut in half lengthwise. Place layers of lamb, potatoes, onions, carrots and kidneys in a casserole, seasoning each layer with salt and pepper and ending with potatoes on top. If oysters are used, layer along with other ingredients. Blend cornflour with cold stock; pour over all. Drizzle with melted butter. Cover tightly with lid and cook in a 275°F oven for 2-1/2 to 3 hours.
Serves 6 to 8

PORK CISTE

3 pork kidneys
vinegar
6 thick pork chops
1/2 pound pork liver, chopped
2 medium onions, sliced
1 large carrot, sliced
1 tablespoon chopped parsley
1/2 teaspoon thyme
1 bay leaf
salt and freshly ground pepper
about 3/4 pint beef stock
1 recipe ciste pastry (following)

Soak and clean kidneys according to Steps I and II in basic instructions, using vinegar in soaking liquid; drain and slice into bite-size pieces. Place chops vertically around inside edge of medium saucepan. Fill center of pan with kidneys, liver, onions, carrot and seasonings. Pour in stock just to cover the vegetables. Cover and simmer gently for 30 minutes.

In the meantime, prepare pastry. Roll out to fit diameter of saucepan. Lay pastry over vegetables, allowing rib bones to pierce pastry. Press to fit snuggly against the vegetables. Pan should be deep enough to allow for at least an inch of rising. Cover and cook gently over low heat for 1 hour. Serve in the saucepan. Loosen edges with sharp knife and cut into 6 wedges.
Serves 6
Note: This dish may also be cooked, uncovered, in a 375°F oven for 1 hour or until crust is golden.

Variation: Follow the above recipe, substituting all lamb meats for the pork. As per basic instructions, lamb kidneys need not be soaked.

CISTE PASTRY

8 ounces flour
4 ounces kidney suet, very finely
    chopped
1 teaspoon baking powder
1/2 teaspoon salt
6 to 8 tablespoons milk

Combine flour, suet, baking powder and salt in a bowl. Cut with pastry blender until mixture resembles small peas. Add enough milk to make a soft but manageable dough. Roll out on a pastry board to desired size.

TRIPE, ETC.

Although the definition of tripe is often confined to stomachs of ruminants only (even-toed, hoofed animals with a three- or four-chambered stomach such as the cow, sheep, deer, etc.), here tripe refers to the edible stomach of any butchered animal. Tripe has long been a mainstay of man's diet but it has been a food representing extremes. In Paeolithic times, before the advent of pottery and bronze, the stomach paunch of a hog might have been used as a cooking vessel. Stuffed with the hunter's kill, it was waterproof and heatproof enough to be hung over an open fire. The nomadic Scythians, likewise, followed this procedure. The herdsmen stripped the flesh from an animal, packed it into the stomach bag and then cooked the entire thing over a fire made from the dried bones of the animal. (Some stomachs had a capacity of 30 to 40 gallons, depending on the animal — sheep, goats, horses or cattle.) Other nomads, wandering tribesmen of the Gobi desert, prepared braised camel's paunch or roasted camel's hump — slaughtering their beasts of burden only after they were too old to work.

A pig's paunch, served in vinegar and the herb silphium, was a delicacy of ancient Greece. In fact, Callimedon, a notorious contemporary gourmand, was ridiculed about his intense love for tripe. It was said that while most men would be willing to die for their country, Callimedon undoubtedly would give up his life for a boiled paunch. And rennet, a derivative of the stomach lining, was used by the Greeks, as well as by the Romans, Arabs and others, for curdling cheese, a practice which remains today.

Tripe rose in popularity in the Italian kitchen in the late 1300's and has been popular ever since. In 15th century Italy a potage made of tripe was served, and *busecca,* a rich thick tripe soup from Lombardy has become one of the best-known tripe dishes of today.

There was a popular preparation of tripe in Northern Europe in the 18th century. A concoction made with blood, a good quantity of fat, some flesh, lungs and heart, it was packed into a stomach paunch and suspended over the fire to cook. The Scots have their version of this dish called haggis, made with either deer or, today more commonly, sheep. The animal's liver is mixed with other ingredients and stuffed into the stomach paunch to cook. It is traditionally brought in to the music of bagpipes and eaten with mashed swedes, potatoes and nips of whiskey.

During the 18th century in America, pepper pot soup, most often identified with the Pennsylvania Dutch, was created by the head chef of the Revolutionary Army forces to save George Washington's troops from starvation at Valley Forge. With the gift of several hundred pounds of tripe from a nearby butcher and pepper-corns donated by a Germantown patriot, the hearty "belly-comforting" pepper pot was invented, sharing the glory of a victory over the Red Coats.

Tripe is also part of the Eskimo diet. They regard the partially digested contents of the stomach as a special treat, possibly because of the flavor resulting from the fermentation.

Intestines, the long series of tubes connecting the stomach with other organs, have likewise been savored by many throughout history. After the conquest of Mexico, Bernal Diaz reported seeing, on the market stalls of the Aztec capital of Tenochtitlan, cooked foods, giblets and "tripas" ("tripas" being synonymous with the guts or entrails of the wild deer, the most commonly butchered animal of the day). These stalls may be regarded as the forerunner of the French triperie, where tripe and other offal may be purchased, including intestines, calf's and sheep's heads. brains, sweetbreads, udders, feet, tongue, heart, liver, spleen and kidneys.

In the United States, the slaves on the plantations in the South were given left-overs from the master's house which included chitterlings (small pork intestines). Chitterlings, or chitlins, soon became one of the most revered Southern dishes. Intestines, specifically the margut (intestines of an unweaned calf), were essential to the "son-of-a-bitch" stew of the cowboys of the Western plains. Although what went into the stew depended on the trail chef, the addition of margut and the cook-ing of it over a fire of buffalo chips made it authentic.

Today, intestines are eaten in a variety of ways in many cultures — the stuffed and spit-roasted kid or lamb intestines of Greece and Italy; cordula, seasoned spit-roasted lamb intestines of Sardinia; and, of course, their use as casings for all kinds of sausages. One of the most succulent preparations for intestines comes from Hawaii. A pig is starved for two weeks, then fed only rice for one week. The pig is killed and roasted, never having been dressed. The intestines, stuffed with rice, are eaten along with the flesh and innards of the animal.

PREPARATION OF TRIPE

Tripe in its broadest sense may refer to the edible stomach of all butchered animals. More specifically it has been used to refer only to the stomach of ruminants, even-toed, hoofed animals that have a 3- or 4-chambered stomach, including the cow, sheep, etc. In this book we use the term tripe in recipes only when referring to the stomach of a cow, which is sold in pieces rather than whole. There are generally 2 types of beef tripe available from your butcher. That which comes from the walls of the paunch or rumen (the large first compartment of the stomach of a ruminant) is called plain or flat tripe. It has a slippery texture. The other kind of tripe, which comes from the walls of the reticulum (the second stomach of a ruminant), is referred to as honeycomb tripe, named so because of its honeycomb-like appearance.

All tripe from the butcher is very white. This is a result of the lengthy and tedious processing (soaking in lime, then in brine and boiling, much the same as the process for olives) that is completed before its arrival on the wholesale-retail market. Be aware that the subsequent cooking times vary considerably, depending on the extent of this processing.

Flat and honeycomb tripe are interchangeable in the recipes that follow, unless otherwise noted. Honeycomb tripe is usually more tender than the flat variety, and requires at least 30 minutes less cooking time. Adjust cooking times in recipes accordingly. Although the stomach of a sheep or pig may be referred to as tripe in the broad sense of its being stomach, because it is most often sold whole for stuffing, we have referred to it as stomach rather than tripe. These animal stomachs have the slippery texture of flat or plain tripe.

Step I: Cleaning and Parboiling

Wash tripe well, rub with salt and rinse thoroughly. Then, if called for in recipe, parboil tripe in salted water (1 tablespoon salt per 1-1/2 pints water) for 15 minutes. Drain, discarding water. Proceed with recipe.

A pig's or sheep's stomach is generally cleaned the same way as tripe. However, remaining membranes and excess fat should be removed from the lining. Turn the stomach inside out for stuffing. Parboiling of a stomach may or may not be necessary, depending on the particular recipe.

Step II: Court Bouillon

Place tripe in court bouillon to cover and simmer, covered, for 1 to 3 hours, or until tender, depending on size of pieces and extent of precooking. Reserve stock for soup base and stews if not to be used in the recipe. Proceed with recipe.

Ingredients for court bouillon:
1 onion, stuck with 2 cloves
2 stalks celery with tops
3 to 4 sprigs parsley
1 carrot
1 bay leaf
8 peppercorns
1 teaspoon thyme (optional)
water to cover

GRILLED TRIPE

Following Steps I and II in basic instructions, clean, parboil and cook tripe until tender, about 1-1/2 hours. Drain. Cut into bite-size pieces. Dip into flour, then into melted butter and finally into fine French bread crumbs. Grill, smooth side up, for 3 to 4 minutes; turn and continue grilling until nicely browned. Serve with tartare sauce or lemon wedges.

FRIED TRIPE

The preparation is simple. Following Steps I and II in basic instructions, clean, parboil and cook tripe until tender, about 1-1/2 hours. Drain and cut into strips. Roll in fine French bread crumbs and drop into hot oil. Or if you prefer, the pieces may be dipped in beaten egg, then rolled in bread crumbs and fried. It's important to maintain the oil temperature, so don't fry too many pieces at once.

Variation: Rather than deep-frying tripe, sauté tenderly cooked strips of tripe in melted butter, after dusting individual pieces with flour. Sauté equal proportions of sliced green peppers and sliced onions in a separate pan. Combine tripe with onions and green peppers in a dish and pour a Bechamel sauce over all (page 133).

PEPPER POT SOUP

3 pounds honeycomb tripe
1 veal knuckle
2 onions, chopped
1 bay leaf
1 stalk celery, including top
2 leeks, including tops, cut in half
2 sprigs parsley
1 sprig thyme
1 tablespoon salt
1 teaspoon freshly ground black pepper
dash of cayenne
1 or more dried red chilis, finely
    chopped
4 potatoes, peeled and diced
1 green pepper, seeded and diced
2 tablespoons chopped parsley
5 tablespoons flour
1/2 pint evaporated milk
2-1/2 to 3 ounces butter

Clean and parboil tripe according to Step I in basic instructions; cut into 1/2-inch dice. Place veal knuckle, onions, bay leaf, celery, leeks, parsley, thyme and 6-1/2 pints water in a large stock pot. Bring to a boil and skim any scum that rises to the top. Simmer, covered, 2 hours.

Strain broth; then remove meat from knuckle bone and dice. Return meat to pot along with tripe, salt, pepper, cayenne and chilis and simmer, covered, 1-1/2 hours longer. Add potatoes, green pepper and parsley; cook another 20 minutes. Blend flour and milk together; gradually add to the soup mixture until slightly thickened. Add butter. Serve very hot in large bowls with plenty of crusty bread.
Serves 8 to 10

TRIPE & POTATO SOUP

2 pounds tripe
1/4 pound bacon or fat salt pork, in
    one piece, blanched and diced
2 stalks celery, including tops,
    chopped
2 onions, chopped
1 carrot, scraped and diced
1 bay leaf
salt and freshly ground pepper to taste
1 small cabbage, shredded
4 potatoes, peeled and diced
2 leeks, chopped

Clean and parboil tripe according to Step I in basic instructions. Rinse in cold water; drain. Cut into 1/2-inch dice. Sauté bacon in a frying pan until fat runs. Add celery, onions and carrot; cook for 5 minutes. Place bacon mixture in a stock pot with the tripe, bay leaf and a little salt and pepper. Cover with 5 pints water and simmer 1 hour. Add cabbage, potatoes and leeks to the stock and adjust seasonings. Simmer, covered, 1 hour longer. Serve very hot.
Serves 6

BEAN CURD SOUP WITH PIG'S STOMACH AND TAILS

1 pig's stomach
2 pigs' tails, cleaned and cut in
   1-1/2-inch pieces
8 dried Chinese mushrooms*, soaked
   to soften and sliced
1 1-inch piece choong toy*
   (preserved turnip – optional)
10 Chinese red dates*
1 teaspoon salt
1/4 pound dried bean curd*, soaked
   to soften and cut in 2-inch
   lengths, or
1 pound fresh bean curd*, cut in
   1-inch squares

Clean pigs' tails according to Step I in basic instructions for preparation of tails. Prepare pig's stomach according to Step I in basic instructions, parboiling tails at same time; drain, discarding water. Return both meats to pot and cover with 4 pints fresh cold water. Add mushrooms, preserved turnip, Chinese dates and salt and bring to a boil. Reduce heat, cover and simmer for 2 hours until stomach is tender.

Remove stomach, add dried bean curd and continue cooking for 30 minutes; if fresh is used, cook only 15 minutes Slice stomach into 1/2x2-inch pieces; return to pot. Heat through and serve. The pigs' tails and stomach are delicious as a side meat dish, dipped in soy or Chinese oyster sauce.*

Serves 6 to 8
*Available in Oriental stores.

MENUDO

The Mexicans are convinced menudo is one of the best panaceas for a hangover. Though we cannot attest to this fact, we feel it is one of the greatest pots of soup (which can likewise be made into a stew). An authentic menudo is made with mixtamal hominy, white fermented corn, but it is also delicious in this version, which substitutes chick peas.

2 calf's feet, or
1 veal knuckle
4 pounds tripe
2 onions, chopped
4 cloves garlic, finely chopped
1 tablespoon crushed oregano
2 tablespoons chopped fresh coriander
salt and freshly ground pepper to taste
1 pound chick peas, soaked overnight

Wash calf's feet and simmer in 9 pints water in a covered stock pot for 1 hour. (This step may be eliminated if veal knuckle is used, as it goes in with the tripe.) Wash tripe and cut into 1x2-inch pieces, or smaller. Add tripe to calf's feet along with onions, garlic, oregano, coriander, salt and pepper. Bring to a boil, cover, reduce heat and simmer for 3-1/2 to 4 hours. After 2-1/2 hours, add the chick peas, which have been soaked overnight and drained. (Canned chick peas need only be heated through at the last moment.) Serve, providing dishes of chopped onions, chopped fresh coriander and hot chili peppers for each person to his liking.
Serves 10 to 12.

GOLDEN TRIPE

2-1/2 pounds tripe
approximately 1-1/4 pints court bouillon
1 clove garlic, finely chopped
6 to 8 tablespoons finely chopped
  parsley
4 tablespoons olive oil
1/4 pound bacon, finely chopped
1 onion, thinly sliced
salt and freshly ground pepper to taste
4 eggs
5 tablespoons freshly grated
  Parmesan cheese

Wash tripe; cook in court bouillon according to Step II in basic instructions, about 1-1/2 hours. Drain, reserve stock and cut into 1-1/2-inch squares. Sauté garlic and parsley in 2 tablespoons olive oil until garlic is golden. Remove with slotted spoon. Add the remaining oil, bacon and onion slices and sauté until onions are limp. Add garlic mixture, tripe, salt and pepper. Simmer 2 to 3 minutes. Add 1/4 pint reserved stock; cover and cook over low heat about 30 minutes. Just before serving, beat eggs together with Parmesan cheese. Pour this mixture over tripe; stir lightly and cook just until eggs are set, about 1 or 2 minutes. Mixture should have a creamy consistency. Serve immediately.
Serves 6

CURRIED TRIPE STEW

2 pounds tripe
3 tablespoons peanut oil
2 cloves garlic, finely chopped
1 slice fresh ginger root,
  finely chopped
1 onion, sliced
1 8-ounce can tomato sauce
1/2 pint chicken or beef stock
1 to 2 tablespoons curry powder
1 teaspoon salt
1/2 teaspoon white pepper
4 carrots, peeled and cut in chunks
1 green pepper, cut in chunks
fresh coriander for garnish

Clean and parboil tripe according to Step I in basic instructions. Drain; cut into 1-inch dice. Heat oil in pan; add garlic, ginger and onion and sauté. Add tripe and a little more oil if necessary; sauté until lightly browned. Then add tomato sauce, stock, curry powder, salt and pepper. Bring to a boil, cover and simmer 1 hour. Add carrots and continue to cook 25 minutes. Add green pepper and cook 10 minutes longer. Garnish with coriander. Serve with steamed rice.
Serves 4 to 6

TRIPE GRATINÉE

2-1/2 pounds tripe
4 tablespoons diced bacon
1 onion, sliced
1 sprig rosemary
1 pint beef stock
4 ounces button mushrooms, sliced
4 tablespoons butter
6 toasted French bread rounds,
  dried out in the oven
freshly grated Parmesan cheese

Wash, clean and parboil tripe according to Step I in basic instructions. Drain; cut in thin strips. Sauté bacon in large frying pan to render fat. Add onion and cook until lightly browned. Add tripe and rosemary and cook for 5 minutes. Add stock and simmer slowly for 1-1/2 hours or more, until tripe is very tender, adding more stock if necessary. Sauté mushrooms in butter 3 minutes. Add to the tripe the last 15 minutes of cooking time.
In the meantime, prepare bread rounds. Place each slice in individual ovenproof serving dishes. Add tripe with its broth and sprinkle with Parmesan cheese. Place under grill a few minutes until golden; serve immediately with crisp green salad.
Serves 6

TRIPE WITH SAUSAGE

2 to 3 calf's feet, split

1/2 pound chorizo or other spicy
    pork sausages

3 pounds tripe

1 small unpeeled garlic bulb*

2 small bay leaves

3 sprigs parsley

2 large onions, chopped

1/4 pound raw cured ham, cut into
    1/2-inch dice

1 onion, chopped

2 cloves garlic, chopped

2 tablespoons olive oil

3/4 pound tomatoes, peeled, seeded,
    and chopped

1 or more dried hot red chilis,
    finely chopped

1 teaspoon paprika

salt and freshly ground pepper to taste

Clean and parboil calf's feet according to Steps I and II of basic instructions for preparation of feet. Clean and parboil tripe following instructions in Step I of tripe preparation. Cut tripe in 1-1/2-inch squares. Prick sausages several times with a fork and simmer in a little water for 5 minutes. Drain and set aside.

Tie garlic bulb, bay leaves and parsley loosely in a cheesecloth bag. Place in a large flameproof casserole along with the tripe, calf's feet, 2 large chopped onions and 5 pints water. Bring to a boil, cover and simmer 2 hours. Add ham and simmer another hour.

In the meantime, sauté the chopped onion and garlic cloves in olive oil until onion is transparent. Add tomatoes, chilis and paprika; reduce over high heat until liquid has almost entirely evaporated. Combine this mixture with some of the stock from the casserole and then pour mixture slowly back into the casserole, stirring constantly. Slice sausages and add to pot; continue to cook, partially covered, for another 15 minutes. Remove the cheesecloth bag. Adjust seasoning with salt and pepper. Serve piping hot with lots of crusty French bread.

Serves 6 to 8

*This means a whole head, not a single clove. It contributes a subtle aroma to the pot.

TRIPE WITH HARICOT BEANS

3 pounds tripe
4 tablespoons butter
4 tablespoons diced salt pork, blanched
6 small onions, finely chopped
1 stalk celery, chopped
2 carrots, chopped
1 sprig sage
1 14-ounce can Italian plum tomatoes,
    chopped
salt and freshly ground pepper
1/2 pint beef stock
1/2 pound dried haricot beans,
    soaked and cooked
freshly grated Parmesan cheese

Wash, clean and parboil tripe according to Step I in basic instructions; drain and cut into narrow strips. Continue with Step II; drain. Heat butter and salt pork over medium heat. Sauté onions, celery, carrots and sage until golden brown. Add tomatoes and cook for 10 minutes. Then add tripe, salt, pepper and stock. Bring to a boil, reduce heat and cook 30 minutes. Add beans and adjust seasonings. Continue cooking 10 minutes longer. Serve with Parmesan cheese.
Serves 6

TRIPE ESPANOLE

3 pounds tripe
1 onion, chopped
4 tablespoons olive oil
2 cloves garlic, mashed
1 can (14-ounce) peeled tomatoes,
    chopped
1 bay leaf
salt and freshly ground pepper to taste
1 teaspoon crushed oregano
1 dried hot red chili, seeds removed
    and finely chopped
1 4-ounce jar pimientos, cut in pieces

Wash tripe and cut into long strips. Cook according to Step II in basic instructions, about 45 minutes; drain. In the meantime, make tomato sauce. Sauté onion in olive oil until transparent. Add garlic, tomatoes, bay leaf and remaining seasonings; simmer, covered, for 15 minutes. Remove bay leaf. Add tripe to sauce and cook until tender, about 1 hour. Add pimientos just before serving.
Serves 8

Variation: Prepare Tripe Espanole as directed. Spoon onto slices of toasted, buttered bread. Then sprinkle with grated hard mild Cheddar and Parmesan cheese. Garnish with sliced black olives and place under grill until golden. Makes a rich winter luncheon entrée.

TRIPES À LA MODE DE CAEN

This is one of the world's classic recipes and probably can be singled out as the most famous of all innard recipes. It requires long, long, slow cooking. Short cuts definitely cannot produce the same results. In France, this dish used to be baked in communal ovens. Today it may be purchased ready to eat at the charcuterie.

5 pounds honeycomb tripe, cut
   in 1-1/2-inch squares
2 calf's feet
1/4 pound salt pork, blanched and
   sliced
2 cloves garlic, finely chopped
4 onions, sliced
3 leeks, sliced
5 carrots, sliced
4 stalks celery, sliced
salt and freshly ground pepper to taste
bouquet garni (page 132)
3/4 pint dry white wine
1/4 pint Calvados or dry cider
beef stock
chopped parsley for garnish

Prepare tripe according to Step I in basic instructions, cutting after parboiling. Prepare calf's feet according to Step I for preparation of feet; split and chop into 3-inch lengths. Line a large earthenware casserole with the salt pork. Then arrange alternate layers of the vegetables and tripe. Salt and pepper each layer and place bouquet garni about in the middle of the casserole. Place the calf's feet on top. Add wine, Calvados and stock to fill the casserole. Cover with a tight-fitting lid. Cook in a 250°F oven for 8 to 10 hours, or overnight. Remove the bouquet garni and serve bubbling hot with French bread. Serves 8 to 12

TRIPE MARMITE

This dish is much like tripes à la mode de Caen, but requires less cooking.

2-1/2 pounds honeycomb tripe
2-1/2 pounds pigs' feet, cleaned
2 leeks, chopped
2 carrots, chopped
2 stalks celery, chopped
2 onions, sliced
2 sprigs parsley, chopped
2 cloves garlic, finely chopped
salt and freshly ground pepper to taste
1/4 teaspoon freshly ground nutmeg
1/8 teaspoon ground cloves
1/2 teaspoon thyme
1/2 pint beef stock
1/2 pint dry white wine
2 tablespoons butter
1/2 pound mushrooms, sliced

Prepare tripe according to Step I in basic instructions; cut into 1-1/2-inch squares. Prepare pigs' feet according to Step I in preparation of feet. Split and chop into 3-inch lengths. Combine vegetables. Mix salt, pepper, nutmeg, cloves and thyme together. Put a layer of tripe and pigs' feet into a large flameproof casserole; top with a layer of vegetables and sprinkle with seasonings. Repeat until all ingredients are used. Pour stock and wine over all, adding more in equal amounts if necessary to cover. Bring to a boil, reduce heat, cover and simmer over very low heat for 4 hours.

Heat butter in saucepan and sauté mushrooms for 2 to 3 minutes; add to casserole last 15 minutes of cooking time. Skim off any fat and serve very hot with French bread and wine. Serves 8

TRIPE VINAIGRETTE

Following Steps I and II in basic instructions, clean, parboil and cook tripe until tender, about 1-1/2 hours. Drain. Cut into strips and cover with vinaigrette dressing (page 132). Chill well. Good served as an hors d'oeuvre or first course.

Variation: Substitute sauce Gribiche (page 133) for the vinaigrette dressing.

HAGGIS

To many a Scotsman, haggis conjures up fond memories, this being the national dish of his homeland. The traditional haggis is made from a sheep's pluck (heart, lungs and liver), mixed with finely chopped suet, oatmeal and onions, then stuffed into a sheep's paunch (stomach bag) and boiled. Though haggis as such is passionately acclaimed as Scottish, similar dishes – many of them of ancient origin – appear in most traditional peasant cuisines throughout Europe. Nevertheless, haggis has been immortalized by Robert Burns in his lines To a Haggis (1786) and is eaten at least once a year by his countrymen at Rabbie Burns' night suppers.

1 sheep's stomach
1 sheep heart
1 sheep liver
1/2 pound fresh suet
3 ounces pinhead oatmeal
3 onions, finely chopped
1 teaspoon salt
1/2 teaspoon freshly ground pepper
1/4 teaspoon cayenne
1/2 teaspoon nutmeg
generous 1/4 pint stock

Wash and parboil stomach according to Step I in basic instructions. Put in cold salted water for several hours. Cover heart and liver with cold water, bring to a boil, reduce heat, cover and simmer for 30 minutes. Chop heart and coarsely grate liver. Toast oatmeal in a heavy frying pan over moderate heat, stirring frequently, until golden. Combine all ingredients and mix well. Loosely pack mixture into stomach, about two-thirds full. Remember, oatmeal expands in cooking.

Press any air out of stomach and sew up securely. Put into boiling water to cover. Simmer for 3 hours, uncovered, adding more water as needed to maintain water level. Prick stomach several times with sharp needle when it begins to swell; this keeps the bag from bursting. Place on a hot platter, cut open and serve very hot with a spoon. Ceremoniously served with "neeps and nips"–mashed turnips, nips of whiskey and mashed potatoes.

PIG'S STOMACH
BRAISED IN SOY SAUCE

1 pig's stomach*
generous 1/4 pint soy sauce
4 tablespoons sugar
4 tablespoons dry sherry
1/2 teaspoon chinese 5-spice powder*
1 whole star anise*
2 slices fresh ginger root
1 piece dried tangerine peel*
2 spring onions with tops, cut up
2 sprigs coriander (optional)

Prepare pig's stomach according to Step I in basic instructions, parboiling for 10 minutes. Discard water. Bring 3/4 pint water to a boil with remaining ingredients; add pig's stomach, reduce heat, cover and simmer for 1-1/2 hours until stomach is tender. Turn stomach over every half hour to insure even flavoring and coloring. When tender, lift out stomach and cut in 1/2x1-1/2-inch strips; reserve juices for other uses. Garnish with some extra spring onion and coriander, if desired. Serve hot or at room temperature.
Serves 6
*If it is impossible to get a pig's stomach, substitute 2 to 3 pounds tripe in one piece, cleaned and parboiled according to basic instructions.
**Available in Oriental stores

Note: The reserved juices should be strained, put into a glass jar and stored in the refrigerator. Use for flavoring meats or vegetables in stir-frying or reuse in braising or marinating other meats such as pigs' feet, tails or ears, tongue, chicken and duck feet.

STUFFED PIG'S STOMACH,
CHINESE STYLE

1 pig's stomach
2 slices fresh ginger root
1/4 pound glutinous rice*
1/4 pound water chestnuts, chopped
6 dried Chinese mushrooms*, soaked to soften and diced
6 to 8 tablespoons diced smoked ham
1 piece dried tangerine peel*, soaked and finely chopped
3 tablespoons peanut oil
1/4 pint chicken stock
2 tablespoons soy sauce
2 tablespoons dry sherry
6 to 8 tablespoons chopped spring onions and tops
1 teaspoon fried sesame oil**
peanut oil for deep-frying
soy sauce
dry mustard

Following instructions in Step I, wash and clean pig's stomach, removing membranes and excess fat from lining. Cook in salted water with ginger slices for 1-1/2 hours, or until tender. Drain and pat dry with paper towels. (Reserve stock for later use, such as bean curd and pigs' tail soup.) Cook rice and keep hot.
Sauté water chestnuts, mushrooms, ham and tangerine peel in the oil for 2 minutes. Add stock, soy and sherry; cover and simmer for 10 minutes. Add spring onions and sesame oil, then combine with hot cooked rice in a large bowl. Toss well.
Fill the pig's stomach and truss, catching edges securely. Place oil in wok or deep cooking vessel and heat until very hot. Deep-fry stomach until crisp and golden on both sides. Drain; let rest 5 minutes. Slice and serve with soy sauce and hot mustard.
Serves 6 to 8
*Available at Oriental stores
**This is the dark seasoning oil available at Oriental stores

STUFFED SOW'S MAW

Whenever there was a sow to be slaughtered, there was a sow's maw to be stuffed, according to the Pennsylvania Dutch. You may not be willing to take it from the beginning, but your butcher may rescue one for you.

1 pig's stomach
1 pound minced pork
1 pound pork sausage meat
4 raw potatoes, peeled and
    finely diced
1 onion, chopped
2 stalks celery, chopped
1/4 teaspoon marjoram
1/4 teaspoon ground sage
1/2 teaspoon pepper
1/2 pint dry cider
1/2 pint beef stock

Following directions in Step I, wash and clean pig's stomach, removing membranes and any excess fat from lining; pat dry with paper towels. Combine all other ingredients except liquid and pack loosely in stomach; truss or secure with skewers. Place on a rack in a shallow roasting tin; pour cider and stock over, cover with foil and roast in a 325°F oven for 3 hours. Uncover last half hour, basting skin until it is crisp and golden brown. Remove trussing string or skewers; cut in thick slices with a very sharp knife. Serves 6 to 8

PREPARATION OF INTESTINES

Intestines are used in braising, stewing and frying (as in chitterlings) almost as much as they are used for casings. The way you plan to serve them, of course, will determine the variety and size. Pork, lamb and beef intestines, all can be eaten. However, pork intestines are most commonly used for casings. Generally speaking, there are 3 categories of pork intestines. The small, sheer pork intestines are used to encase fresh sausages or thin sausages such as Italian dry salami. The caecum, called the *sac* or *poche* in French, is slightly larger and expands to about 1-1/2 to 2 inches when stuffed and cooked or dried, as in the French *andouilles.* The colon, or *chaudin,* is the largest intestine and is used in the making of *andouilles* and other sausages.

Intestines for both casings and cooking unstuffed may be used fresh or partially cooked. Casings that are purchased partially cooked may also be preserved in a brine or salted down. These must be soaked to soften and to remove saltiness. Although this book uses only innards in the forcemeats, forcemeats made of any ingredients may be prepared and loosely stuffed into any variety of intestine to make sausage.

Step I: Cleaning
To clean intestines, first cut them into manageable lengths, about 1 to 2 feet. Then run cold water through the opening, using a funnel or faucet nozzle, until water runs clear. Remove any excess fat.

If intestines are to be used other than for sausage-making, they may be slit lengthwise and cleaned. Although we suggest that you clean the intestines before using, many ethnic cultures prefer them to be left alone. The undigested food within the intestines is regarded as a delicacy, much like the tomalley of the lobster and crab "butter."

Step II: Soaking
Soak intestines at least 1 hour in a bath of 1 tablespoon salt or baking soda to 1-1/2 pints water. Rinse well again and proceed with recipe.

Cooking Time
Pork and beef intestines require 2 to 4 hours of simmering; veal and lamb intestines are more tender and therefore require only 2 hours of simmering at the most. If intestines are used for casing in sausage-making, cooking time is further reduced because the skin is stretched considerably in stuffing. (See boudin, page 87, for directions on preparing and cooking sausages.)

CHITLINS

Hog's jowls, collard greens and chitter-lings or chitlins (the small intestines of a hog) are probably the most famous of all soul food.

5 pounds chitterlings
3 cloves garlic
1 lemon, halved
1 teaspoon freshly ground pepper
2 whole cloves
1 teaspoon thyme
2 sprigs parsley
2 bay leaves
2 onions, quartered
1 teaspoon salt
1/4 teaspoon mace
1/4 teaspoon allspice
1 tablespoon marjoram
4 tablespoons cider vinegar
1/2 pint tomato sauce or thick fresh
   tomato purée
cayenne to taste

If chitterlings are purchased pre-cooked, prepare according to Step II in basic instructions; if they are pur-chased fresh, prepare according to Steps I and II. Place chitterlings in a large pot with water just to cover; add all ingredients except tomato sauce and cayenne. Simmer, covered, for 3 to 4 hours, or until tender. (Timing will vary depending whether fresh intestines or partially cooked chitter-lings are used.) During the last 30 min-utes of cooking, add tomato sauce and cayenne. Serve with coleslaw and corn bread.
Serves 8 to 10

Variation: Follow the preceding recipe, omitting cloves, mace, allspice, marjoram, vinegar, tomato sauce and cayenne. Add 2 stalks celery and 2 or more dried hot red chilis, crushed, to cooking liquid. After chitterlings are tender, drain well, pat dry and cut into 2-inch squares. Dip in beaten egg and roll in cornmeal, and fry in hot deep fat. Drain on paper towels. Serve with Tabasco sauce.

BULGARIAN BAKED LAMB INTESTINES

2 pounds lamb intestines
3 carrots, scraped and sliced
1 stalk celery, sliced
3 sprigs parsley
2 tablespoons butter or vegetable oil
8 spring onions, whites only, chopped
3 cloves garlic, finely chopped
2 to 3 tomatoes, seeded and chopped
3 eggs
1 tablespoon flour
1/2 pint yoghurt
freshly grated Parmesan cheese

Prepare intestines according to Steps I and II in basic instructions. Put in a pot with carrots, celery, parsley and 3/4 pint water. Bring to a boil, reduce heat, cover and simmer 45 minutes. Strain vegetables, reserving stock. Cut intestines into 1-inch pieces and set them aside.
Heat butter in a frying pan. Sauté onions and garlic until transparent; add tomatoes and cook 3 to 4 minutes lon-ger. Place mixture in a 2-1/2-pint baking dish; add intestines and 1/4 pint reserved stock. Bake at 350°F for 20 minutes. Beat eggs, flour and yog-hurt together and pour over intestines; Sprinkle with Parmesan. Return to 400°F oven and bake until firm and golden, about 10 minutes.
Serves 6

BURRITOS DE TRIPAS

An American cook might put minced beef, possibly boiled beef, into burritos, but the Mexicans use pork and tripas more commonly in theirs. (Tripas in Spanish refers to any section of the digestive tract, from the plain tripe to the actual intestines, which are often braided together in long strands before cooking.) In San Francisco there are restaurants that specialize in burritos filled with these meats. First the meats are cooked in huge pots of simmering lard that has been seasoned with a salt-water brine until very tender. (Water allows lard to boil; salt will not dissolve in lard.) Then they are chopped and placed into the tortillas. Cooking the meat this way not only retains the juices, but makes them very tender and flavorful, but not the least bit greasy.

lard
tripe or intestines (usually pork)
tortillas (page 134)
hot refried beans (page 135)
Mexican rice (page 135
hot tomato sauce (page 133)

Clean tripe according to Step I in basic instructions. If using intestines, prepare according to Step I in basic instructions for intestines. In a large pot, melt enough lard to cover tripe. Add at least 1/2 pint water in which some salt has been dissolved. Bring to rolling boil, being careful hot fat does not splatter on you. Add tripe and simmer over low heat, uncovered, for 2 to 3 hours until tender. Meat will not be crisp. Drain well and blot with paper towels; chop meat. Place meat, refried beans and rice along with sauce to taste in center of warm tortilla; roll up.

Variation: Tongue may be cooked and used in this manner also.

TRIPAS DE LECHE

Mexicans regard this dish as one of the greatest of all delicacies. The *tripas de leche,* known also as the milk intestines or marrow gut, refers to the tubular canal connecting the stomachs of an unweaned calf. Needless to say, they are very tender and require little cooking.

The intestines are washed, cut into 2-inch lengths and then slowly deep-fried in lard until crisp. They may also be roasted or grilled; however basting is essential to avoid drying out. By tradition, they are eaten with tortillas (page 134) and a tomato sauce (page 133).

CHARCUTERIE

Though *charcuterie* in French literally means a shop where one buys cooked meats prepared in a wide variety of ways, pork in particular, we feel the definition of the art of charcuterie should include any forcemeat stuffed into any intestine or stomach. By using this broader definition, charcuterie might have commenced in Paleolithic times with stuffing a filling into a stomach paunch and cooking it. Men of all cultures have been preserving meats, making forcemeats and "stuffing" for a very long time.

A banquet dish known in India in the first millenium B.C., called *mandaliya,* was actually a sausage made from entrails stuffed with spices and marrow and roasted over an open fire. Then in medieval times, cooked foods such as forcemeat and baked meats made their first appearances in marketplaces. These items were in the form of sausages as well as terrines. Today, the French have their *andouille* and *boudin* (coinciding with the pig slaughter); the Germans have their *weisswurst* and *bockwurst*; the Turks and Greeks have their *kukerets* or *kokoretsi*, made of lamb intestines that have been wrapped around finely chopped heart, kidney, liver and sweetbreads and seasoned with oregano, dill, lemon juice and olive oil; the Poles have their *kielbasa*; the Italians have their *mortadella*; and the Spanish have their *chorizo.* The Israelis have a different method of preparing sausages; they stuff the necks of poultry — of turkey, chicken, goose or duck.

The recipes within this chapter are limited to forcemeats or stuffings made with offal. We hope you will use your imagination to create others.

CHARCUTERIE SPICE

Every merchant in France has his special blend of quatre-épices (four spices). Likewise, we've blended our own. However, we've expanded it to include five spices.

4 tablespoons freshly ground white
    pepper
1 tablespoon freshly grated nutmeg
1 tablespoon ground ginger
1/2 teaspoon cinnamon
1/2 teaspoon ground cloves

Combine all ingredients and store in a jar with a tight-fitting lid.

FROMAGE DE TÊTE VINAIGRETTE

2 calves' heads
pickling brine (page 132)
1 bay leaf
6 whole cloves
6 peppercorns
1/2 teaspoon powdered sage
4 to 8 tablespoons wine vinegar
8 tablespoons thinly sliced pimento-
    stuffed olives
1/2 teaspoon freshly ground pepper
vinaigrette dressing (page 132)

Remove eyes, brains, ears, snouts and most of fat from heads. Soak in several changes of cold water to remove blood. Place in pottery or glass crock, cover with salt brine and store in a cool, dark place for 7 to 10 days. Cover with cold water and parboil for 15 minutes; discard water. Return to pot with fresh cold water, bring to a boil and add bay leaf, cloves, peppercorns, sage and vinegar. Reduce heat, cover and simmer for 3 to 4 hours until meat comes away from bones.
Remove heads from pot and remove and chop all meat from bones. Strain and reduce stock to 1-1/2 pints. Cool and chill until partially set. Then stir in pepper, olives and chopped meat. Pour into an oblong mould. When set, cut in strips or slices. Serve with vinaigrette, garnished with chopped parsley, chives or spring onions.
Serves 10 or more

CHOPPED CALF LIVER

1 1-pound piece calf liver
4 tablespoons butter
1 large onion, finely chopped
6 to 8 tablespoons chopped parsley
1 teaspoon salt
1/2 teaspoon freshly ground pepper
1/4 teaspoon freshly grated nutmeg

Bake liver in a 325°F oven for 30 minutes. Cool, remove membranes and veins; chop finely. Heat 2 tablespoons butter and sauté onions and parsley until onions are transparent. Mix with liver and chill briefly. Blend with remaining butter. Season with salt, pepper and nutmeg. Pack into crock or mound on lettuce leaves. Serve with thin slices of rye bread.
Serves 4

Variation: Follow the above recipe, adding 1/4 teaspoon tarragon, fresh lemon juice to taste and 1 chopped hard-boiled egg.

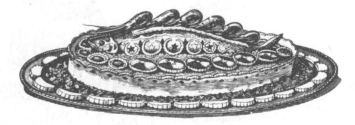

POTTED PORK LIVER PÂTÉ

1 pound pork liver, membranes removed
1 pound lean pork
1 pound pork fat
salt and freshly ground pepper
1 clove garlic, finely chopped
2 tablespoons finely chopped shallots
1/4 teaspoon charcuterie spice
   (page 83)
1 pound pig's caul*
strips of pork rind as needed
1/2 pint dry white wine
6 to 8 tablespoons brandy
4 to 5 marrow bones, cut in
   1-inch pieces
2 large carrots, sliced
1 onion, sliced
1 bouquet garni (page 132)

Mince together coarsely the meats and fat. Season with salt and pepper to taste. Add garlic, shallots and charcuterie spice and mix well. Spread a piece of pork caul flat on the table. Put the minced meat mixture in the center. Wrap the caul around it and bring the ends together, forming into a large mound.

Line an earthenware casserole with pork rind, fat side up. Place mound in casserole and moisten with wine and brandy. Surround with marrow bones and vegetables; submerge bouquet on the side. Bake, uncovered, in a 250°F oven for 2-1/2 hours, basting fre-quently with cooking liquid. When the mound is well glazed and meat is done, remove and cool. Chill. Serve at room temperature.

Note: If pâté is not to be eaten within a week, remove to clean earthenware casserole or terrine and cover with melted pork fat to 1 inch above pâté. Tie greaseproof paper or foil over the top; cover. May be stored up to a month in the refrigerator.
Serves 8 or more
*Pig's caul is the fatty, net-like membrane investing the intestines, sometimes available on request from a good butcher.

PAUL'S PÂTÉ

2 pounds chicken livers
4 tablespoons vegetable oil
1 large dill pickle, cut in chunks
1/2 onion, cut in chunks
1/2 green pepper, cut in chunks
2 hard-boiled eggs, finely chopped
1 teaspoon prepared mustard
1 teaspoon paprika
1/2 teaspoon freshly ground pepper
1 or more teaspoons salt
2 tablespoons mayonnaise

Sauté livers in oil until firm; drain on paper towels. Then mince livers, using a medium blade, with pickle, onion and green pepper. Mix well with remaining ingredients. Pack in pottery crocks.
Serves 8

QUICK LIVER PÂTÉ

1/2 pound liver sausage, at room
   temperature
3 ounces unsalted butter,
   at room temperature
1 tablespoon grated onion
1 tablespoon chopped chives
2 tablespoons finely chopped parsley
2 tablespoons brandy
salt and freshly ground pepper

Cream together the liver sausage and butter. Add remaining ingredients and form into a smooth mound or pack into crocks.
Serves 4

CHICKEN LIVER TERRINE

1/2 pound chicken livers
4 tablespoons butter
1 onion, cut in chunks
2 cloves garlic, finely chopped
1 pound minced pork
2 eggs, beaten
1/2 teaspoon charcuterie spice
   (page 83)
1/2 teaspoon rosemary or thyme
2 teaspoons salt
1/2 teaspoon freshly ground pepper
4 tablespoons brandy
6 to 8 tablespoons pistachio or pine nuts
3 tablespoons flour
blanched bacon slices or salt pork
   strips as needed
1 bay leaf

Sauté livers in butter until firm. Set aside and let cool. Then mince with onion and garlic, using a fine blade. Combine with remaining ingredients. Line terrine with overlapping bacon slices and press mixture into it. Cover with bacon slices and place bay leaf in center. Cover with a tight-fitting lid and bake in a 350°F oven for 1 to 1-1/2 hours, or until liquid in dish and fat run clear. Cool 15 minutes, then weight down and cool thoroughly. Store in refrigerator, but serve at room temperature.
Serves 6

COUNTRY TERRINE

1 pound lean pork, minced
1 pound pork liver, chopped
2 pounds minced veal
3/4 pound smoked tongue, diced
4 tablespoons brandy
1 pound fat pork, diced
1 teaspoon each marjoram and basil
2 tablespoons chopped parsley
1 clove garlic, finely chopped
1 teaspoon charcuterie spice (page 83)
1 teaspoon each salt and freshly
   ground pepper
blanched bacon slices as needed
1 bay leaf

Mix together the minced pork, liver and veal, and put them through the mincer once more. Marinate tongue in brandy for 30 minutes. Mix together all ingredients until well blended. Line a large earthenware baking dish or terrine with overlapping bacon slices. Pack mixture in dish and top with bacon slices; place a bay leaf in center. Bake in a 350°F oven for 1-1/2 to 2 hours, or until fat runs clear. Cool and chill. Serve at room temperature.
Serves 10 or more

ANDOUILLE

The charcuteries of France are filled with andouilles and andouillettes (the smaller variety)—a dry pork sausage commonly made from pork tripe, even heart and spleen, and put in a pig-intestine casing. Butchers, in fact, are acclaimed for their individual recipes. Andouilles, made from large pig intestines, are most often eaten cold as hors d'oeuvre (cut in thin slices as salami), whereas the andouillettes made from small intestines are usually served hot, accompanied by sautéed or mashed potatoes or braised sauerkraut.

The sausages are first poached in lightly salted water and allowed to cool. They are then lightly slashed, brushed with butter and grilled or fried. The most famous of these sausages come from Troyes, Tours, Vire, Nancy, Strasbourg, Caen and Lyons, to mention only a few. Our recipe is similar to the sausages from Nancy because the spleen and heart are included in the forcemeat.

5 pounds pork trimmings from
    neck, including blood if possible
1 pork heart
1 pork spleen
1-1/2 tablespoons salt
1 tablespoon freshly ground pepper
1 teaspoon charcuterie spice
  (page 83)
1 onion, finely chopped
4 cloves garlic, finely chopped
6 to 8 tablespoons chopped parsley
large pork intestines
sea salt

Mince meats, using a medium blade. Add remaining seasonings and mix well. Put in a crock and store in a cool place overnight. Stir well the next day and stuff the intestine three-quarters full; tie off in 12-inch lengths. Roll in sea salt and let stand in salt 8 to 10 days. Remove from salt and hang to dry for 2 months. To serve, simmer in lightly salted water for about 1-1/2 hours (see procedure for boudin, page 87). Serve warm or chilled.
Makes 8 to 10 pounds sausage

Variations: This same mixture may be stuffed in small pork intestines to make andouillettes; reduce the cooking time. Or wrap the mixture in a double-thickness of pig's caul (see instructions for potted pork liver pâté, page 84); do not salt or hang to dry.

BLACK PUDDING

1 pork heart
1 pound pork spleen
2 pounds pork kidneys
1/2 pound pork fat or fat belly pork
2 to 3 pounds pork trimmings from butt or neck, including blood if possible
6 to 8 tablespoons dry sherry
2 teaspoons crushed oregano
1 teaspoon caraway seeds
1/2 teaspoon dill
1 tablespoon salt
1-1/2 teaspoons coarsely ground pepper
1 pound pork intestines for casings

Clean and prepare pork intestines (see Steps I and II, intestines, page 79); soak in water until ready to use. Prepare heart and kidneys according to basic instructions (see pages 37 and 55, respectively). Remove membranes from spleen.

Mince meats, including fat and trimmings, using a medium blade. Then combine with remaining ingredients and mix well. Fill the intestines three-quarters full, using a sausage stuffer to simplify the procedure. Tie off in desired lengths. Hang sausages in well-ventilated, cool room for 2 to 4 hours to blend flavors. Place in refrigerator overnight.

Cook either by boiling (see instructions for boudin below), grilling or frying. Cooking time varies, depending on thickness of sausage. Serve with sautéed apple rings, braised sauerkraut and boiled potatoes. Or serve on pumpernickel bread with hot mustard and thinly sliced onion rings.
Makes 6 to 7 pounds sausages

BOUDIN
(Blood Sausage)

1/2 pound pork fat, cut in 1/4-inch dice
2 large onions, finely chopped
1/2 pint rich beef stock
2 tablespoons lard
2 tablespoons flour
3/4 pint evaporated milk or fresh milk and single cream, mixed
1-1/2 pints fresh pork blood, strained through a fine sieve
1 teaspoon charcuterie spice (page 83)
1 tablespoon very finely chopped parsley
2 ounces button mushrooms, very finely chopped and sautéed in
1 tablespoon butter
pork casings (page 79), cut in 18-inch lengths

Combine pork fat, onions and stock in large saucepan. Bring to a boil, reduce heat, cover and simmer 1 hour. In another saucepan melt lard. Blend in flour and gradually add milk, stirring constantly.

Continue cooking until sauce begins to thicken. Stir in onion mixture. Bring to a boil and simmer 10 minutes, stirring constantly. Remove from heat and pour all at once into pork blood. Add charcuterie spice, parsley and cooled mushrooms.

Have ready 18-inch lengths of cleaned casings, tied at one end with white string. Fill casings three-fourths full with blood mixture, using a funnel (3/4 inch in diameter) to facilitate filling. Tie open end with string. To cook, drop prepared sausages, a few at a time, into boiling salted water; simmer gently for 25 minutes, uncovered. Prick any sausages that rise to the surface with a pin to allow air to escape, thus preventing sausages from bursting. Remove sausages with a slotted spoon and let cool. Refrigerate. (Sausage may be stored up to 3 days in the refrigerator, or frozen.)

To serve, make diagonal slashes in the skin of the sausage and grill over hot charcoal. Or, sauté, unslashed, in a little butter and oil. Serve with sautéed apple slices or on a bed of braised sauerkraut.
Makes about 5 pounds sausages

GALANTINE OF CHICKEN

1 4-1/2-pound roasting chicken
2 teaspoons salt
2 tablespoons butter
1 onion, chopped·
1 pound minced veal
1/2 pound chicken livers, diced
1 slice bread, soaked in
2 tablespoons milk
2 hard-boiled eggs, finely chopped
2 eggs
4 tablespoons Port or Madeira
2 tablespoons chopped chervil
4 tablespoons double cream
1 teaspoon paprika
salt and freshly ground pepper
1/2 pint dry white wine
2 cloves garlic
1 carrot, sliced
3 sprigs parsley
lemon slices, parsley and radishes
    for garnish

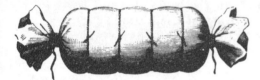

Bone chicken as follows. Lay it, breast side down, on a cutting board. With a small, sharp, thin-bladed knife, cut the skin down the backbone. Keeping the point of the knife tight against the bones, gradually separate meat from bone down one side almost to the breast bone, using shallow strokes and taking care not to pierce the skin. Remove wing at the shoulder and drumstick at the knee, making the smallest possible holes in the skin. Sever hip joint internally and remove the thigh bone with a single lengthwise slit on the inside and a gradual cutting away from the bone. Repeat procedure for other side. Lay the almost detached meat flat on either side and carefully cut meat away from the breast bone, taking care to avoid slitting the skin and keeping the skin and meat in one piece. Chop extracted meat and rub inside skin well with salt. Heat butter and sauté onion until transparent. Add veal and livers. Combine this mixture with chicken, bread, eggs, port, chervil, cream, paprika, salt and pepper.

Lay chicken skin open flat on a table. Heap forcemeat in center and truss with white string. (This procedure is more easily handled if another person holds raw skin together while you are sewing.) Brush well with melted butter. Tie securely in muslin or cheesecloth, tying in several places to hold the shape. Place in a large pot with wine, garlic, carrot, parsley sprigs and 3/4 pint water. Simmer gently for 1 hour or until tender, turning once. Remove from heat and let cool in stock. Carefully remove to platter and chill overnight. To serve, garnish with lemon slices, parsley and radishes. Remove wings and legs and then cut into crosswise slices.
Serves 8 to 10

Variation: When galantine is chilled, decorate with triangles of hard-boiled egg white, pimiento strips and green beans. Make an aspic by dissolving 1 tablespoon powdered gelatine in 3/4 pint clarified chicken stock; heat stock and then add juice of 1 lemon in which 1/2 teaspoon tarragon leaves have been steeped, then strained out. Set pan of hot stock in a bowl of ice until the aspic becomes syrupy. Brush the partially set aspic over the galantine and chill. Pour leftover aspic into a shallow dish to make a layer about 1/4 inch thick. Chill until set; chop and surround gelatine with chopped aspic.

STUFFED PIG'S FEET

The French, Italians and Chinese stuff the entire foreleg of the pig. We have used just the pig's foot, which is more economical.

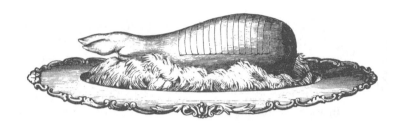

2 pig's feet, skin intact
court bouillon to cover (page 93)
1/2 pound brains (any kind), cleaned
    and parboiled 10 minutes (page 7)
4 tablespoons chopped parsley
4 tablespoons brandy
2 tablespoons soft bread crumbs
1/2 teaspoon charcuterie spice
   (page 83)
3 tablespoons pistachios
3 tablespoons chopped mushrooms
2 tablespoons chopped shallots
1 egg
1 teaspoon salt
1/2 teaspoon freshly ground pepper

Choose large meaty pig's feet with skin intact. Slit underside of pig's feet just to the toes. Carefully remove meat and bones, leaving toes undisturbed and skin intact. Soak the skins in cold water to cover and 1 tablespoon salt for 1 hour, or until ready to use. Boil meat and bones in court bouillon to cover for 1-1/2 hours until tender; remove from pot. When cool enough to handle, remove all meat and gelatinous parts; chop finely and combine with remaining ingredients.

Pat the skins dry; sew cut edges together with white string, forming a tube. Stuff with prepared forcemeat and re-form into original shape. Wrap each foot separately in several layers of cheesecloth, covering the opening well to prevent mixture from bursting out. Wrap several times again and tie in several places to hold shape. Place in a large pot so feet lie flat on the bottom. Cover with boiling water, return to the boil and simmer for 1-1/2 hours. Do not unwrap. Cool, then chill. Unwrap just before slicing. A spectacular culinary coup de maître.

Variation: Follow the preceding recipe, substituting 3/4 pound minced pork and pork casings for the pig's feet. Fill casings (see page 79) and cook in simmering water for 35 minutes (see instructions for cooking boudin).

HEADS, FEET & TAILS

The heads of animals have, in the past, been honored with pageantry by nobility, yet eaten by peasants in grateful acceptance of God's gift of nourishment. They have been roasted over open fires, boiled for rich, gelatinous stocks and cleaned of their flesh for brawn or forcemeats.

It is an ancient custom in China for the fish head to be served to the oldest (and most honored) member of the family; the cheeks and soft pockets behind the eyeballs are regarded as the greatest delicacy of all. This custom was also prevalent in 19th century France, when the carp's head was served to the most distinguished guest at the table, although the French considered the tongue of the carp to be the juiciest morsel of all.

In medieval England, the boar's head was a dish served at grand banquets. The arrival of the head (previously roasted and decorated) was heralded by trumpeters, with ladies and gentlemen of the court parading joyously behind. This tradition became associated with Christmas and there's even an old English Christmas carol written in praise of the boar's head. The ceremony is still celebrated at Queen's College in Oxford and has even spread to California: at the Awahanee Hotel's Christmas dinner in Yosemite National Park, a boar's head is symbolically presented to the company.

A 15th century Italian cookbook gives a recipe for calf's head dipped in garlic juice, and states that all heads of four-footed beasts are heavy foods, but nourishing, and work wonders for increasing male fertility. Alexis Soyer, the great chef who set up kitchens to aid Florence Nightingale in the Crimean War, and who wrote *A Shilling Cookery for the People,* created several very delicious recipes for sheep's heads. Pigs' cheeks were also prized in England. They were first smoked, then boiled in seasoned water and served cold.

In France during the early 1800's, one of the most fashionable dishes of the day was calf's head served in its hide. The eyes were thought to be the most tantalizing, then jowls, temples, ears and tongue; each of these was served with a small portion

of the brain. Curiously enough, there was such an overabundance of sheep's heads in Argentina in the late 1800's that they were actually used to fill potholes and ruts in the roads.

A present-day delicacy in Turkey is known as *bash*. A sheep's head is roasted until crisp, then brought to the table and cracked open before all who are present. The brain is brought out first, then the tongue, followed by the other meats.

Tails, snouts, ears and feet have all shared a bit of culinary eminence, too. The Sumerian tribes (about 4000 years ago) developed a breed of sheep called fat-tailed sheep, noted for an especially fat tail which represented about one-sixth of the sheep's total body weight. A single tail might weigh as much as 10 pounds and was a rich source of high-quality fat — unquestionably the delicacy of the time. The sheep's tail achieved even greater fame in the pastoral society of Baghdad; *alya*, fat rendered from the sheep's tail, was the basis of practically every dish.

The nose or snout of an animal made a contribution to the kitchen when a dog was used in Babylonian times to unearth a kind of truffle from the ground. In France, this important task is performed by pigs, not dogs. Led on truffle-hunting expeditions, the pig gained stature in man's mind because he could find food as well as be used for food. De la Reynière, a famous epicure, mourned over the dishonor generally paid to the pig, saying: "Everything in a pig is good. What ingratitude has permitted his name to become a term of opprobrium?"

The Puerto Rican fishermen also had great respect for the pig's nose. Pigs were always carried in a ship's hold when the sail plan took them out of sight of land. When it came time to return to port, the pig was brought on deck and used as a compass, for he invariably pointed his snout toward land. The Romans' affection, however, was exhibited in a different manner. The pig to them was a culinary masterpiece. They ate the paunch, testicles, matrix, cheeks, ears, snout, feet, entrails and cracklings, as well as the fat. This culinary appreciation of the pig persisted throughout history — especially in China, England, France and even America. Many Americans are familiar with Pennsylvania Dutch scrapple or ponhause — a mixture of cornmeal, pork trimmings and spices. Benjamin Franklin is also known to have waxed enthusiastic about pigs.

Trotters or feet have been an important part of many cuisines. When cooked, they produce gelatine, a nutritious substance high in protein that sets when it cools. Pigs' trotters were a favorite of the ancient Greeks and Romans. The Chinese ate them along with all appendages, accurately believing they strengthened the body.

Consommé has been made from calf or poultry feet since the 15th century in Italy. One recipe called for pheasant, partridge or pigeon feet combined with cinnamon, sage and other spices. The Italians thought consommé healthy for old and hearty alike. And, of course, it was indispensable to *haute cuisine,* when there was an *à la gelée* of everything.

Pieds de Porc St.-Menehould is probably the most famous of all French preparations of feet. It is said that this dish was indirectly responsible for Louis XVI's death. It was during a fateful stop to fill his belly with pigs' feet in the village of St.-Menehould that he was recognized by Jean-Baptiste Drouet, a member of the Convention, and apprehended, later to be beheaded.

In America, "pocket soup" or "portable soup" was one of the main foods of explorers and travelers. A forerunner to the bouillon cube, it was actually concentrated stock made from veal trimmings and pigs' trotters. Nowadays, pigs' feet are generally available in most markets; however, sheep's trotters are more difficult to find. In the United States, for example, sheep's trotters are commonly rendered into fertilizer, used for tallow material or sent to the glue factory rather than sold on the retail market for food.

PREPARATION OF HEADS, FEET, TAILS, EARS AND SNOUTS

The edible foot of an animal is often called a trotter. However, for the sake of clarity, we will call them feet, with one exception: Through common usage, sheep's trotters have become the accepted term for the feet of both lamb and sheep.

Step I: Cleaning

Remove any hairs on heads, feet, tails, ears or snouts by singeing over an open flame or plucking. Scrub well (using a vegetable brush if desired) and then sprinkle with salt, rubbing it into the skin. Rinse well with cool water; pat dry. Remove any excess fat. Poultry feet (chicken, duck or turkey) must be stripped of their outer scaly skin; plunge them in boiling water 1 minute, as you would do before peeling tomatoes. Proceed with recipe.

Step II: Parboiling

Parboil in salted water (1 teaspoon salt to 1-1/2 pints water) for 5 minutes. Drain, discarding water. This step serves the purpose of ridding the meat of congealed blood as well as clinging meat, fat or bone residue, thereby adding clarity to sauces.

Step III: Court Bouillon

Cook in following court bouillon. Bring meat to boil in court bouillon, reduce heat, cover and simmer for 1-1/2 to 3 hours, depending on type and size of meat. Follow recipe instructions for cooking times.

Ingredients for court bouillon:
2 stalks celery, with tops
1 onion, stuck with 2 cloves
1 carrot
8 peppercorns
bouquet garni (page 132)
6 allspice berries (optional)
1/2 lemon (optional)

If the court bouillon is not used as part of the recipe, it may be strained and reserved for a rich soup stock or added to stews and sauces. Note: We prefer adding the lemon to a court bouillon when cooking pigs' feet, snouts, ears or tails as it enhances the flavor and helps cut the richness created by their gelatinous quality.

CALF'S HEAD SOUP

1 calf's head
1 onion, peeled and halved
1 bunch parsley
1 teaspoon crushed marjoram
1 bay leaf
2 tablespoons salt
1 teaspoon grated lemon rind
6 to 8 tablespoons chopped parsley
1 egg
5 tablespoons flour
salt and freshly ground pepper to taste
4 tablespoons vegetable oil
3 tablespoons butter
4 tablespoons dry sherry or Madeira

Wash calf's head well; parboil for 5 minutes in water; drain, discarding water. Return to pot with 5 pints fresh cold water; bring to a boil and simmer for 3 hours, skimming from time to time to remove scum. Then add onion, parsley, marjoram, bay leaf and salt and continue cooking another hour. Strain stock; set aside. Remove all meat from bones.

Make forcemeat by mincing the meat lemon rind and chopped parsley together. Add egg, 2 tablespoons flour, salt and pepper; shape into small balls the size of a walnut. Fry in oil until golden.

Melt butter in soup pot. Stir in remaining 3 tablespoons flour and cook 3 or 4 minutes to brown slightly. Gradually add reserved stock, cooking to thicken slightly. Add sherry just before serving. Return meatballs to soup and serve.
Serves 8

LAMB'S HEAD SALAD

1 lamb's head, whole
1 onion, chopped
1 carrot, peeled and chopped
1/2 celeriac, peeled and chopped
1 bay leaf
1 teaspoon salt
freshly ground pepper to taste
2 tablespoons olive oil
1 tablespoon white wine vinegar
1 tablespoon chopped parsley
1 tablespoon chopped fresh dill
1 teaspoon chopped fresh celery leaves

Cover lamb's head with water and parboil for 10 minutes; discard water. Return to pot with fresh water to cover, adding vegetables, bay leaf, salt and pepper. Bring to a boil, reduce heat, cover and simmer for 1 hour, or until meat falls completely away from bones. Strain cooking liquid and reserve for later use. Cut meat into bite-size pieces, chill and before serving mix with oil, vinegar, parsley, dill and celery leaves.
Serves 6 to 8

Variation: A pig's or calf's head can be prepared in the same way.

LAMB'S HEAD SOUP

For a rich soup, thicken the reserved broth from the preceding recipe with 3 tablespoons cream and 1 egg yolk. Combine cream and egg yolk in a bowl and gradually add a cup of the hot stock. Stir this mixture into remaining stock and heat through.

CRISP ROASTED PIG'S HEAD

1 pig's head, cleaned and
    tongue removed
1 teaspoon Chinese 5-spice powder*
2 tablespoons salt
6 to 8 tablespoons mien see* (ground
    brown bean sauce), or oyster sauce*
4 tablespoons bourbon, scotch or gin
12 ounces honey, combined with
scant 1/2 pint boiling water
watercress or coriander
    sprigs for garnish

Prepare pig's head according to Step I in basic instructions. Place head in a colander in the sink and pour a kettleful of boiling water over. Let cool. Combine the 5-spice powder, salt, bean sauce and alcohol. Slash meat on underside of head and rub half of the spice mixture into the meat. Rub the remaining spice mixture into the skin. Place head upright on a rack in a large roasting tin. Roast at 375°F for 1-1/2 hours. Lower heat to 325°F and continue roasting for an additional 2 hours, or until the meat is cooked through, basting the skin well every 30 minutes with the honey-water mixture. (Cooking time will depend on the size of the head.) If ears begin to brown too quickly during cooking period, wrap them with foil. When head is done, remove to platter and garnish with watercress or coriander. Chop head into pieces and serve with sweet vegetable relish (page 135) or Chinese plum sauce.

Serves 8 or more

*Available in Oriental stores

SHEEP'S HEAD

Sheep's heads traditionally have been served (and relished) by the peoples of sheep-herding countries—from England and Scotland to the Middle East. Unfortunately, as the pastoral life gives way to modern technology, these native dishes are rapidly disappearing.

1 sheep's head
rose water
2 to 3 onions, sliced
salt and freshly ground pepper

Remove snout altogether as it is very difficult to clean. With a sharp knife clean head, scraping carefully; also singe off any hairs. Place head in a pot with water to cover and simmer 30 minutes, skimming away any scum that rises to the surface. Drain; pat dry. Rub with rose water and return to pot. Smother with onions, season with salt and pepper and add fresh water just to cover. Bring to a boil, reduce heat, cover and simmer head for about 3 hours. Serve hot or cold with vinaigrette dressing (page 132).
Serves 3 to 4

ROASTED LAMB'S HEAD

1 lamb's head with tongue, skinned
  and cleaned
5 tablespoons olive oil
4 tablespoons dry red wine
1-1/2 teaspoons crushed oregano
2 cloves garlic, finely chopped
1/2 teaspoon salt
1/2 teaspoon freshly ground pepper

Remove eyes and tongue of lamb's head. Then parboil head in water to cover for 10 minutes. Simmer tongue for 30 minutes in salted water; skin. Return to lamb's mouth.
Make a marinade by combining remaining ingredients; pour over head while warm and marinate for 1 hour, turning occasionally. Bake in a 325°F oven for 1-1/2 hours, basting from time to time. Place on a bed of parsley, surrounded by tiny red tomatoes. Decorate with a garland of daisies. To serve, split head lengthwise with a cleaver. Scoop out brains and carve meat.
Serves 4

SCRAPPLE

A Pennsylvania Dutch-inspired breakfast dish.

4 pounds pork scraps with bones, or
1 pig's head, split lengthwise
1 teaspoon salt
6 peppercorns
3 whole cloves
1 bay leaf
1/2 pound cornmeal
1 onion, finely chopped
1/4 teaspoon cayenne
1/2 teaspoon freshly ground nutmeg
1/2 teaspoon or more ground sage
salt and freshly ground pepper

Parboil pork scraps or head, in water to cover, for 10 minutes. Drain; discard water. Return to pot with fresh water to cover, salt, peppercorns, cloves and bay leaf. Bring to a boil, cover and simmer for 3 hours, or until meat falls off the bones easily. Strain stock; reserve. Remove all meat from bones and chop; set aside.
Reheat stock; gradually add cornmeal, stirring constantly until thick, about 15 minutes. Add meat, onion, cayenne, nutmeg and sage; adjust seasonings with salt and pepper. Pour into 2 greased loaf tins. Refrigerate until set. Slice and fry for breakfast. Will keep in the refrigerator up to 1 week.
Serves 12

THE FAT PIG CASSEROLE

2 pig's ears
2 pig's feet
1/4 pound fat salt pork or bacon
  scraps, blanched
1 pound lean pork, cut in 1-inch cubes
3 tablespoons vegetable oil
2 tablespoons butter
1 onion, thinly sliced
1/4 pint dry white wine
2 stalks celery, finely chopped
2 carrots, finely chopped
1 head cabbage, quartered
3/4 pound cotechino or other spicy
  pork sausages, sliced

Prepare pig's ears and feet according to Step I in basic instructions. Cut ears in half and chop pig's feet roughly with a cleaver; cut salt pork into 1/4-inch slices. Put all meat, except cubed pork, into pot with water to cover and simmer 1 hour. Remove meat with slotted spoon; cut ears into thin strips; remove any loose bones.
Heat oil and butter in a large frying pan. Sauté onion until lightly browned. Add pork cubes and brown on all sides. Add wine, celery, carrots, pig's ears and feet, salt pork and 3/4 pint stock. Simmer for 30 minutes. Place cabbage wedges on top of meat and continue cooking 30 minutes longer. Finally add sausage, cover and cook 20 minutes. Skim off any excessive fat.
Serves 8

PICKLED PIGS' EARS, CHINESE STYLE

2 pounds pigs' ears
4 whole star anise*
3 slices fresh ginger root
6 to 8 tablespoons white wine vinegar
4 tablespoons sugar
1 teaspoon salt

1/2 pint white wine vinegar
1/2 pound sugar
1 tablespoon thinly sliced fresh
   ginger root
3 cloves garlic, sliced
1 teaspoon salt
2 large carrots, sliced
1 cucumber, unpeeled, seeded and
   cut in chunks
1 mild onion, cut in chunks
1 green pepper, cut in chunks

Prepare pigs' ears according to Steps I and II in basic instructions; drain. Return to pot with water to cover and next 5 ingredients listed above. Bring to a boil and simmer 1 hour; let meat cool in liquid. Discard liquid and cut ears into 1/2x1-inch slices.

In the meantime, bring 1-1/2 pints water to a boil with remaining vinegar, sugar, ginger, garlic, salt and carrots. Turn off heat when boiling point is reached. Cool mixture to room temperature. Then add cucumber, onion, green pepper and sliced pigs' ears. Chill in refrigerator for at least 4 hours to blend flavors. Will keep up to 1 week refrigerated. Serve as an appetizer or a cold meat side dish.
Makes 3 pints
*Available in Oriental stores

MORAHAN'S VEGETABLE SLICER.

PIGS' EAR SALAD

1 pound pigs' ears
3 whole star anise*
1 2-inch slice fresh ginger root
2 large carrots, cut in thin julienne
   strips
1 cucumber, peeled, seeded and cut
   in 2-inch julienne strips
2 spring onions, tops only, slivered
   lengthwise and cut in 2-inch
   julienne strips
6 to 8 tablespoons chinese plum sauce*
   or mango chutney, mashed
salt and freshly ground pepper
lemon juice to taste
crisp lettuce leaves
toasted sesame seeds

It is important that all ingredients in this recipe be well chilled. Prepare pigs' ears according to Steps I and II in the basic instructions. Discard water and return ears to pot with water to cover, star anise and ginger. Bring to a boil, reduce heat, cover and simmer for 45 minutes, or until ears are tender. Remove ears, let cool and chill. Cut into very thin strips (1/8 inch).
Combine pigs' ears, carrots, cucumbers and onions and toss lightly with plum sauce. Season with salt and pepper and a little fresh lemon juice if a slightly tart flavor is desired. Serve on crisp lettuce and sprinkle with sesame seeds.
Serves 6
*Available in Oriental stores

BOILED PIGS' FEET

This is a good procedure to follow if you want pigs' feet to remain whole. Wrapping them in cheesecloth not only helps keep their shape, but prevents the skin from breaking during cooking. It is important to keep the court bouillon at a low simmer. Choose smaller pigs' feet if gelatinous qualities are desired; larger feet offer more meat. After pigs' feet are cooked, they may be breaded, braised or served with any number of sauces, from mild to very piquant.

4 to 6 pigs' feet
court bouillon

Clean pigs' feet according to Step I in basic instructions. Wrap securely and tie in cheesecloth. Proceed with Step III, with the court bouillon. Simmer, covered, over low heat 3-1/2 to 4 hours, depending on size. Cool in stock. Remove cheesecloth. Place in dish and cover with stock, if not to be used immediately; otherwise, freeze. Proceed with following recipes.

GRILLED PIGS' FEET
ST. MENEHOULD

This is one of the great classic dishes of France. Traditionally the pigs' feet are wrapped in cheesecloth and simmered for 24 hours, then allowed to stand for another 24 hours until they become so tender that even the bones can be eaten. The following is a simplified version; the meat will be tender, but don't eat the bones!

pigs' feet, precooked in court bouillon
French bread crumbs

Prepare pigs' feet according to preceding recipe for boiled pigs' feet. Roll in bread crumbs and grill or fry until browned on all sides. Serve 1 large or 2 small feet per person, accompanied by a spicy sauce or Dijon-style mustard.

Variations: Follow above recipe, rubbing pigs' feet with olive oil or melted butter before rolling in bread crumbs. Good with tartare sauce, mustard sauce or Madeira sauce.
Follow above recipe, removing bones from pigs' feet before grilling. Dip in beaten eggs seasoned with dry mustard before rolling in bread crumbs. This is also good fried in butter.
Pigs' tails and ears may be prepared using any of the methods given above.

PICKLED PIGS' FEET

4 to 5 pounds pigs' feet
1 Spanish onion, thinly sliced in rings
3/4 pint white wine vinegar
1 bay leaf
6 to 8 peppercorns
4 whole allspice berries
4 cloves garlic, halved
1 or more dried hot red chilis

Prepare and cook pigs' feet according to preceding recipe for boiled pigs' feet. Cool; unwrap and place in jars along with onion rings. Bring 3/4 pint water, vinegar, bay leaf, peppercorns, allspice, garlic and chili to a boil in a saucepan. Pour over pigs' feet and let cool. Place in refrigerator at least 24 hours before using to allow flavors to blend. This will keep up to 1 week, refrigerated.
Serves 6 to 8

Variation: Pigs' ears, snouts or tails may be substituted for the pigs' feet. Follow Steps I and II in basic instruction. These substitutions need not be wrapped in cheesecloth during cooking period.

CHICKEN FEET

Stock made entirely from chicken feet is very rich and gelatinous. The same holds true if chicken feet are added to a prepared chicken broth. Additionally, chicken feet added to any stew during the cooking period further enriches the sauce, thus enhancing the flavor. The best thing, however, is eating the chicken feet that are left. Dip them in a Tabasco-flavored soy sauce and eat as a meat side dish.

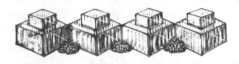

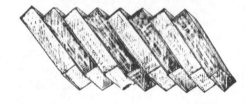

CHICKEN OR CALF'S FOOT JELLY

2 pounds chicken feet, or
2 calf's feet, split
1 onion, quartered
2 carrots
1 stalk celery with leaves
1 clove garlic, crushed
1 teaspoon salt
4 peppercorns
2 bay leaves
2 hard-boiled eggs, sliced
5 tablespoons lemon juice
6 to 8 tablespoons pickles, chopped
lemons, quartered

Prepare feet according to Steps I and II in basic instructions. Place in pot with water to cover, onion, 1 carrot, celery, garlic, salt, peppercorns and bay leaves. Simmer at least 2 hours. Reduce stock to 2-1/2 pints. Strain liquid into mould and set aside to cool. Slice thinly remaining carrot and blanch for 2 minutes. Add carrot along with remaining ingredients to jelled stock. Place in refrigerator until set. Slice for cold cuts or for a first course; garnish with lemon wedges. Cube to serve as an hors d'oeuvre; serve with prepared mustard.
Makes about 2-1/2 pints jelly

Variation: Remove meat from feet, chop finely and add to jelly.

PIGS' FOOT JELLY

A word on pigs' foot jelly. Any court bouillon, in which pigs' feet have been the only meat used, will make a marvelous jelly. (Of course, the same holds true for other feet, such as chicken or calves'.) This jelly is excellent served on salads or sliced into sandwiches or served on a cold buffet table.
Just strain the reserved stock through cheesecloth, add some vinegar or lemon juice to taste and pour into a loaf tin or mould. Chill in the refrigerator until set, about 4 hours. Other ingredients may be added if desired. One of our favorites is the addition of sliced rounds of hard-boiled egg, pimientos and olives to the partially set jelly.

JELLIED PIGS' FEET & TONGUE

3 pig's feet
2-1/2 pints or more court bouillon
1/2 pound smoked tongue, cooked
   and thinly sliced
5 tablespoons dry white wine
5 tablespoons white wine vinegar
5 tablespoons sugar
1/2 teaspoon freshly ground pepper
1/8 teaspoon ground cloves
1-1/2 teaspoons salt
4 tablespoons sliced pimientos (and
   diced, if desired)
watercress

Prepare pig's feet according to Steps I and II in basic instructions. Then cook in court bouillon to cover (2-1/2 pints) according to Step III, about 3 hours or until meat is very tender. Remove feet, reserving stock. Let meat cool. Remove all meat from bones and dice; chill.

In the meantime, reduce stock to 1-1/4 pints. Add wine, vinegar, sugar, salt, pepper and cloves to stock. Bring to a boil and simmer for 5 minutes. Remove from heat, strain, let cool and chill until partially set. Remove from refrigerator; assemble.

To assemble, place a layer of the jellied stock in the bottom of a 2-1/2 pint dish. Layer a few slices of tongue on top, then another layer of jelly with pimientos and diced pigs' feet (reserving some of the more gelatinous pieces for decorating sides and bottom of dish), repeating until all ingredients are used. End with a layer of tongue. Tuck the reserved meat into the sides of the dish. Smooth top with a thin layer of jelly. Chill until set, at least 4 hours. Turn out and serve on a bed of watercress. Slice with a very sharp knife. Serve with Dijon or Pommerol mustard as a first course or on a cold buffet table.

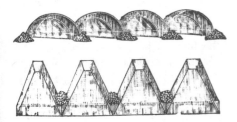

SHEEP'S TROTTERS WITH LEMON SAUCE

12 sheep's trotters
1/4 pint lemon juice
2 tablespoons butter
1 teaspoon chopped fresh mint
2 egg yolks, beaten
salt and freshly ground pepper

Prepare feet according to Steps I and III in basic instructions, simmering in court bouillon. When done, remove all meat from bones and chop. Strain and reserve liquid. Heat 3/4 pint of the reserved stock in a saucepan with lemon juice, butter, mint and meat. Just before serving, combine about 1/2 cup of the heated stock with the egg yolks, stirring constantly; gradually pour egg mixture back into the soup. Cook until smooth and thickened but do not boil again. Season with salt and pepper.
Serves 4 to 6

HOCHEPOT

2 pig's feet, split lengthwise and cut in
   3-inch pieces
1/2 pound pigs' ears
2 pounds beef brisket
1-1/2 pounds veal shoulder
1 pound lamb shoulder
3 sprigs parsley
1 bay leaf
2 sprigs thyme
4 to 6 peppercorns
2 stalks celery, sliced
1 pound Polish boiling sausages
3 carrots, peeled and cut in chunks
12 button onions
2 leeks (tough stems removed), cut
   in chunks
1 head cabbage, quartered
salt and freshly ground pepper
butter

Prepare pig's feet and ears according to
Step I in basic instructions. Put all
meats, except sausages, in a pot and
cover with water. Bring to a boil, skimming away any scum that rises to the
surface. Repeat until all scum has dis-
appeared. Then add herbs and celery,
cover, and simmer for 2-1/2 hours.
Add sausages, carrots, onions and leeks
and continue cooking another 30 minutes. Add cabbage and cook, uncovered, 7 to 10 minutes longer, or until
cabbage is tender. Remove meats and
slice. Place in a warm casserole along
with vegetables and a little of the
stock. Serve with crusty bread.
Serves 10 to 12
Note: Reserve stock for a flavorful
soup base. Meats in the recipe may
vary depending on taste.

Variation: Follow the preceding
recipe, substituting 3 coarsely chopped
onions for button onions. Add 1 turnip
and 2 potatoes, both peeled and cut in
eighths, along with sausages and other
vegetables. After vegetables are tender,
remove with slotted spoon and mash
to a purée, adding a little stock or
double cream to make a smooth consistency. Season with salt and pepper.
Mound in center of warm platter. Surround with sliced meats. Serve at once
with a spicy mustard and pickles.

YUGOSLAVIAN SOUR SOUP

3 pounds pigs' feet, snouts or ears
2 carrots, diced
1 onion, diced
2 stalks celery, diced
1 root celeriac or Hamburg parsley,
   peeled and diced
1 pound potatoes, peeled and diced
2 tablespoons butter or oil
2 tablespoons flour
1 clove garlic, finely chopped
juice of 1 lemon
salt and freshly ground pepper to taste

Prepare meat according to Step I in
basic instructions. Quarter pigs' feet or
cut ears and snouts into bite-size
pieces. Cook meat in 3-1/2 pints water
along with carrots, onion, celery and
root for 1-1/2 hours. If pigs' feet are
used, remove from stock and remove
all meat; dice and return to stock. Add
potatoes and continue cooking 20
minutes longer.
In the meantime, make a roux by first
heating oil in a small saucepan; add
flour and garlic and cook until lightly
browned. Thicken soup with this mixture. Add lemon juice just before serving and adjust seasonings. Serve this
hearty soup with a basket of homemade bread.
Serves 4 to 6

WINTER MELON SOUP WITH DUCK FEET & GIZZARDS

2 pounds winter melon*, pulp
    and seeds removed
1/2 pound duck feet (heads and wings
    may be substituted)
2 dried duck gizzards**, soaked to
    soften (fresh gizzards may be
    substituted)
6 to 8 dried Chinese mushrooms*
    soaked to soften and quartered
    if large
6 to 8 Chinese red dates*
1 piece dried tangerine peel*,
    soaked until soft
2 ounces cooked ham or prosciutto,
    cut in small dice
salt to taste

Scrub skin of the winter melon, but do not remove. Cut in 1-1/2-inch cubes; set aside. Prepare duck feet according to Steps I and II in basic instructions, adding gizzards during Step II. Combine meat with winter melon, mushrooms, red dates and tangerine peel in 5 pints water. Bring to a boil, reduce heat, cover and simmer for 1-1/2 hours until winter melon is soft and transparent. Add ham; adjust seasonings. Serve in soup bowls. Eat winter melon by scooping out flesh with a spoon and discarding skin. Eat the duck feet and gizzards, too.
Serves 6 to 8
 *Available in Oriental stores
**Dried duck gizzards have been salted in order to preserve them (this method has been used by the Chinese for hundreds of years). Before using in any recipe, soak the gizzards in hot water for 15 minutes. To prepare your own dried duck gizzards, salt fresh gizzards liberally. Hang to dry in a warm, breezy area until dried and hard. Store in a glass jar with a tight-fitting lid.

SWEET & SOUR PIGS' FEET SOUP

The Chinese serve this rich, gelatinous soup to post-natal mothers to help them regain their strength. It's spicy, nutritious and warming.

4 pounds pigs' feet, split and halved
    lengthwise
1/2 pint wine vinegar
1/2 pound soft brown sugar
3 tablespoons thinly sliced ginger root
2 teaspoons salt

Prepare pigs' feet according to Steps I and II in basic instructions; drain, discarding water. Return feet to the pot; add fresh water to cover, vinegar, sugar, ginger root and salt. Bring to a boil; reduce heat, cover and simmer 1-1/2 hours, or until pigs' feet are tender. Ladle into bowls and serve hot.
Serves 6 to 8

103

FEET

BRAISED PIGS' FEET

6 pigs' feet, split lengthwise
3 onions, chopped
1 clove garlic, finely chopped
1 green pepper, chopped
2 bay leaves
6 to 8 tablespoons wine vinegar
2 dried hot red chilis, seeds removed
3 stalks celery, chopped
1 4-ounce can tomato paste
1 teaspoon paprika
salt and freshly ground pepper to taste

Prepare pigs' feet according to Step I in basic instructions. Cover with water and cook for 30 minutes; add remaining ingredients. Bring to a boil, reduce heat, cover and simmer for 1-1/2 hours. Serve very hot with rice.
Serves 6

PIGS' FEET AND TRIPE

5 pounds pigs' feet
2 pounds tripe (smooth tripe preferred)
4 strips bacon, cut in 1-inch pieces
2 cloves garlic, finely chopped
2 stalks celery, including leaves, sliced
1 green pepper, diced
6 to 8 tablespoons chopped parsley
1 to 2 dried hot red chilis, seeded and diced
2 teaspoons crushed oregano
2 teaspoons salt
1 teaspoon coarsely ground black pepper
2 bay leaves
1 28-ounce can peeled tomatoes
1/4 pint wine vinegar mixed with 3/4 pint water

Prepare pigs' feet according to Step I in basic instructions; split lengthwise. Clean and parboil tripe according to Step I (page 68); cut into 1-inch squares.

Place pigs' feet in the bottom of a heavy flameproof casserole. Arrange tripe, then bacon, over them and sprinkle with chopped garlic. Mix celery and green pepper with remaining herbs and spices and scatter over surface. Tuck bay leaves into center and pour tomatoes, vinegar and water over all. Bring to a boil, reduce heat, cover and simmer for 2-1/2 hours or until meats are tender. Serve in bowls with French bread or over rice.
Serves 8 to 10

PIGS' FEET & SAUERKRAUT

2 pigs' feet, split lengthwise
3 pounds sauerkraut, rinsed and drained
1 onion, sliced
1 apple, peeled and sliced
1 tablespoon caraway seeds
dry white wine
6 to 8 small potatoes, peeled

Prepare pigs' feet according to Step I in basic instructions. Place a third of the feet in the bottom of a heavy heatproof casserole. Arrange sauerkraut on top. Alternate remaining feet with a layer each of the onions and apples. Top with caraway seeds. Add wine to cover. Cover and simmer until the feet are tender, about 2 hours. Add potatoes and continue cooking 30 minutes longer.
Serves 6 to 8
Note: Frankfurters or pork sausages may also be added to the casserole, allowing just enough time for them to heat through.

TURKISH CALF'S FEET & WHITE BEANS

2 calf's feet, split lengthwise and cut in
    3-inch lengths
4 tablespoons vegetable oil
2 onions, chopped
9 ounces dried haricot beans, soaked
    in water to cover overnight and
    drained
1/2 teaspoon ground ginger
1/2 teaspoon turmeric
1/4 teaspoon cayenne
6 eggs, shells uncracked (optional)*
salt and freshly ground pepper
4 tablespoons chopped fresh coriander.

Prepare feet according to Steps I and II in basic instructions. Heat oil in a flameproof casserole and sauté onions until golden brown. Add the feet and sauté until golden on all sides. Add the beans, ginger, turmeric, cayenne and uncracked eggs. Cover with cold water, bring to a boil, reduce heat, cover and simmer for 2-1/2 hours until meat falls away from bones. Season with salt, pepper and coriander. Serve hot with cucumber and yoghurt salad.
Serves 6
*The eggs are hard-boiled during the simmering of the stew. The whites take up the flavors of the stock and the yolks become very creamy.

CALVES' FEET, ITALIAN STYLE

6 calves' feet
2 tablespoons butter
4 tablespoons olive oil
1 onion, chopped
3 tablespoons tomato paste
1 tablespoon chopped fresh basil
3 tablespoons finely chopped parsley
1/4 teaspoon cinnamon
salt and freshly ground pepper to taste
freshly grated Parmesan cheese

Prepare feet according to Steps I and III in basic instructions, reserving stock. Remove meat from bones and cut into bite-size pieces. Heat butter and oil in a frying pan. Sauté onion until transparent. Add meat, generous 1/4 pint reserved stock, tomato paste, basil, parsley and cinnamon and reduce to half over high heat. Season with salt and pepper. Sauce should be thick. Serve very hot with Parmesan cheese and pasta or polenta.
Serves 6

PIGS' FEET WITH BLACK BEAN SAUCE

2 pounds pigs' feet
2 tablespoons salted, fermented black
   beans (dow see)*, mashed
2 cloves garlic, finely chopped
1 slice fresh ginger root, finely chopped
1 piece tangerine peel*, softened in
   warm water and finely chopped
3 tablespoons oil
2 tablespoons dry sherry
1 tablespoon soy sauce
1/2 pint chicken or pork stock

Clean pigs' feet according to Step I in basic instructions; split lengthwise and cut in half. Continue with Step II; drain. Make paste by mashing together black beans, garlic, ginger root and tangerine peel. Heat oil and immediately add black bean paste and pigs' feet, stirring and browning all the while. Add sherry, soy and stock; bring to a boil, cover and simmer 1 hour, or until feet are tender, but not falling apart. Check liquid from time to time, adding more if necessary to keep meat from burning. Serve with rice and stir-fried greens.
Serves 4

Variation: Chicken feet may be prepared using the same method.
*Available at Oriental stores

PIGS' FEET, KOREAN STYLE

3 pounds pigs' feet
1 teaspoon salt
1 slice fresh ginger root
2 tablespoons peanut oil
2 tablespoons soy sauce
2 cloves garlic, finely chopped
1 tablespoon finely chopped fresh
   ginger root
1/2 teaspoon fried sesame oil*
1 tablespoon toasted sesame seeds,
   crushed
2 tablespoons chopped spring onion
1 dried hot red chili, finely chopped, or
1/4 teaspoon cayenne

Prepare pigs' feet according to Steps I and II in basic instructions; split lengthwise and quarter. (Reserve stock for other use.) Return feet to pot with fresh water to cover, salt and ginger root slice; bring to a boil, reduce heat, cover and simmer for 1-1/2 hours, or until tender. Remove pigs' feet and pat dry. Heat oil and stir-fry pigs' feet until golden brown. Then add soy, garlic, chopped ginger root, sesame oil, sesame seeds, spring onion and chili. Cover, let steam rise to the top and serve with rice.
Serves 6
Note: Use reserved stock for a good soup, adding watercress and cubed bean curd; or Chinese cabbage and spring onions; or spinach and mushrooms.
*This is the dark seasoning oil available at Oriental stores.

PIGS' FEET WITH PLUM SAUCE

3 pounds pigs' feet, left whole
1/4 pint wine vinegar
1 teaspoon salt
2 tablespoons sugar
3 whole star anise*
1 teaspoon fennel seeds
Chinese plum sauce*
preserved ginger
spring onions

Prepare pigs' feet according to Steps I and II in basic instructions; drain, discarding water. Return to pot with water just to cover, vinegar, salt, sugar, star anise and fennel seeds. Cover and simmer for 1-1/2 hours. (It is very important that the pigs' feet do not boil as it will break the skin and cause the meat to separate.) Remove feet from pot, drain and let cool. Then chill in refrigerator. When chilled, split in half lengthwise with a sharp cleaver and chop into 2-inch pieces.

Dip into plum sauce when eating and serve with pickled ginger and spring onions. Serve as an entrée, first course or at a picnic.

Serves 4 to 6

*Available at Oriental stores.

BRAISED CHICKEN FEET
WITH HOISIN SAUCE

2 pounds chicken feet
2 tablespoons hoisin sauce*
1 clove garlic, finely chopped
1 piece dried tangerine peel*,
   soaked to soften and finely chopped
1 teaspoon chopped fresh ginger root
1 tablespoon soy sauce
2 tablespoons dry sherry
1 teaspoon sugar
3 tablespoons peanut oil
1 tablespoon cornflour, blended with
4 tablespoons water

Prepare chicken feet according to Step I in basic instructions. Combine hoisin, garlic, tangerine peel, ginger, soy, sherry and sugar in a bowl. Heat oil in a wide, heavy frying pan until hot and add chicken feet; stir well. Add the hoisin mixture, continuing to stir and browning lightly for 5 minutes. Add 1/2 pint water, cover, reduce heat and simmer for 35 minutes. Bind juices with cornflour mixture. Serve with rice and green stir-fried vegetables.
Serves 4 to 6
*Available at Oriental stores

CHINESE FRAGRANT
BRAISED DUCK FEET

1-1/2 pounds duck feet
2 tablespoons soy sauce
2 tablespoons dry sherry
1 tablespoon sugar
1/2 teaspoon Chinese 5-spice powder*
1 teaspoon finely chopped fresh
   ginger root
1 clove garlic, finely chopped
1 piece dried tangerine peel*,
   soaked to soften and finely chopped
3 tablespoons peanut oil
1 tablespoon cornflour, mixed with
4 tablespoons water
chopped fresh coriander and spring
   onions for garnish

Prepare duck feet according to Step I in basic instructions. Combine soy, sherry, sugar, 5-spice powder, ginger, garlic and tangerine; marinate duck feet in this mixture at least 2 hours; drain, reserving marinade. Heat oil in a large, heavy frying pan and brown duck feet. Combine the marinade with 1/2 pint water; add to pan. Bring just to a boil, cover and simmer 1 hour. Bind juices with the cornflour mixture. Garnish with coriander and spring onions.
Serves 4 to 6
*Available at Oriental stores

Variation: For fried and steamed duck feet, marinate duck feet as above. Drain feet well, reserving marinade. Fry duck feet in hot, deep oil until brown; drain. Then place in a shallow pyrex or ceramic baking dish. Sprinkle 1 tablespoon of the reserved marinade over all and steam in large, covered pot or steamer above 2 inches of water for 40 minutes. Serve with rice and stir-fried greens.

TOSTADAS WITH PIGS' FEET & BEANS

1/2 recipe hot refried beans
(page 135)
12 tortillas, fried crisp (page 134)
6 to 8 tablespoons grated dry mild
Cheddar cheese
shredded lettuce
3/4 pound chopped meat from
pickled pigs' feet (page 99)
2 avocados, sliced
6 to 8 radishes, sliced
1 onion, thinly sliced
hot tomato sauce (page 133)

Spread beans over the tortillas.
Sprinkle with cheese and shredded lettuce. Garnish with chopped meat, avocado slices, radishes and onion. Pour
tomato sauce over all. Serve the tortillas
flat on plates. Alternatively, the beans
and their garnish may be folded up in
the tortillas and eaten with the fingers,
but in this case do not crisp-fry them.
Serves 6

MINCEMEAT

approximately 2-1/2 pounds calves'
or pigs' feet
5 pounds apples, peeled, cored and
finely chopped
1-1/2 pounds currants, washed and
drained
1-1/2 pounds raisins
2 pounds soft brown sugar
1 pound suet, finely chopped
1-1/2 pints cider
3/4 pint brandy
1 teaspoon whole cloves
1 whole nutmeg, freshly grated
1/2 pint orange juice
3 tablespoons grated orange rind
5 tablespoons lemon juice
1 tablespoon grated lemon rind
3 ounces chopped candied orange peel
3 ounces chopped candied lemon peel
6 ounces chopped candied citron
1/2 teaspoon freshly ground pepper
1 teaspoon salt

Prepare feet according to Steps I and
II in basic instructions cooking in
salted water until tender, about 1-1/2
hours. When cool enough to handle,
remove bones and press meat through
a colander. When cold, press through
colander once again.
Meat should resemble pearl barley.
Mix meat thoroughly with all other
ingredients (except salt and pepper).
Store in refrigerator for 3 days to
blend flavors before using. Then divide
between containers and freeze. Use as
needed. Add salt and pepper to mincemeat just before using for pie filling.
Enough for 12 pies; use at least 3/4
pint mincemeat for each 9-inch pie.

PIGS' TAILS & BUTTER BEANS

12 pigs' tails, cut in 2-inch pieces
1 pound butter beans, washed and
    soaked overnight
1 onion, sliced
1 clove garlic, finely chopped
2 green peppers, sliced
1/2 teaspoon dry mustard
1 whole dried hot red chili
4 tablespoons chopped parsley
salt and freshly ground pepper to taste

Prepare pigs' tails according to Step I
in basic instructions. Place in a pot and
cover with water; simmer for 1/2 hour,
skimming to remove any scum. Add all
other ingredients. Cook another 1 to
1-1/2 hours until tender.
Serves 8

Variation: Pigs' ears and feet may be
substituted for the pigs' tails; just prepare particular meats according to basic
instructions for cleaning.

BARBECUED PIGS' TAILS

*We attribute this recipe to the Men-
nonite colony of Ontario. It's often
served at picnics and is known as one
of the favorite foods at stag parties.*

2 dozen pigs' tails
2 tablespoons olive oil
1/2 pint tomato sauce or thick fresh
    tomato purée
4 tablespoons tomato paste
4 tablespoons soft brown sugar
2 tablespoons wine vinegar
1 teaspoon Worcestershire sauce
juice of 1 lemon
1 clove garlic, finely chopped
1 teaspoon dry mustard
salt and freshly ground pepper to taste
1/2 teaspoon rosemary (optional)

Prepare pigs' tails according to Step I
in basic instructions; cut in 3-inch
pieces. Place pigs' tails on a rack and
bake in a 300°F oven for 2 to 3 hours,
until meat is tender and most of fat
has baked off. An alternate method to
this is to simmer the pigs' tails in
acidulated water for 1-1/2 hours. Combine all other ingredients for barbecue
sauce, coating tails well. Grill over hot
charcoal, turning and basting, until
crisp. If fresh rosemary is available,
break off several branches, tie them
together and use as a basting brush.
For barbecuing, we prefer leaving the
tails uncut or halved, so as to have
fewer pieces to keep turning.
Serve with traditional barbecue accompaniments such as corn-on-the-cob,
French bread and green salad.
Serves 6 to 8

OXTAIL CASSEROLE

3 pounds oxtails, disjointed
2 tablespoons bacon drippings or butter
1 teaspoon salt
1/2 teaspoon freshly ground pepper
1 garlic clove, finely chopped
1 onion, chopped
1 carrot, chopped
1 celery stalk with leaves, chopped
1/2 teaspoon thyme
1 bay leaf
3/4 pint dark beer or ale
2 tablespoons malt vinegar
chopped parsley

Prepare oxtails according to Steps I and II in basic instructions. In a flameproof casserole, brown the oxtails in the bacon drippings or butter. Add the remaining ingredients except the malt vinegar and parsley. Cover and simmer for 1-1/2 hours or until meat is tender. Just before serving, stir in vinegar and garnish with parsley. Serve with plain boiled potatoes or boiled noodles.
Serves 4 to 6

OXTAIL & VEGETABLE SOUP

3 pounds oxtails, disjointed
1 bay leaf
1 onion, chopped
2 leeks, chopped
2 stalks celery with leaves, chopped
3 carrots, scraped and diced
3 turnips, peeled and diced
3 beetroots, peeled and diced
2 large tomatoes, peeled and chopped
1/2 pound cabbage, spinach or Swiss
    chard, chopped
2 sprigs parsley, chopped
2 teaspoons salt
1/2 teaspoon freshly ground pepper

Prepare oxtails according to Step I in basic instructions. Place in a large stock pot with 5 pints water. Bring to a boil, skimming to remove any scum that forms. Add the remaining ingredients; cover and simmer for 1-1/2 hours or more. Adjust seasonings and remove bay leaf. Serve in large soup bowls with the oxtails.
Serves 6

Variations: The oxtails may be removed from the stock, drained, dipped in butter, rolled in good French bread crumbs and grilled until crisp.
Pigs' tails may be substituted for the oxtails—just as delicious.

OXTAIL & CHICK PEA CASSOULET

3 pounds oxtails, disjointed
3 tablespoons olive oil
2 cloves garlic, finely chopped
1 onion, chopped
3/4 pint beef stock
1/4 pound fresh fennel, including
   tops, chopped
1/2 teaspoon crushed oregano
salt and freshly ground pepper to taste
1/4 pound ham, cubed
1/2 pound chick peas, soaked overnight
   and cooked until soft

Prepare oxtails according to Step I in basic instructions. Heat olive oil in a flameproof casserole, add garlic and onions, and sauté until transparent. Add oxtails, stirring until they have changed color. Add stock, fennel, oregano, salt and pepper. Cover and simmer 1-1/2 hours. Add ham and chick peas; continue cooking another 30 minutes. Serve hot with French bread and green salad.
Serves 4 to 6

OXTAILS BOURGUIGNON

4 pounds oxtails, disjointed
seasoned flour
1/4 pound bacon, parboiled for
   5 minutes and diced
1/2 pint beef stock
1/2 pint dry red wine
bouquet garni (page 132)
2 tablespoons butter
1/4 pound button onions
1/4 pound button mushrooms
3 carrots, scraped and cut in
   small chunks
6 to 8 tablespoons fresh peas
salt and freshly ground pepper to taste
chopped parsley

Prepare oxtails according to Steps I and II in basic instructions; dredge in seasoned flour. Heat bacon in a flameproof casserole, stirring to prevent browning, but allowing fat to be rendered; remove bacon pieces to side. Add the oxtails to the fat and brown well; drain off any excess fat. Return bacon pieces to casserole along with stock, wine and bouquet garni.

Heat butter and sauté onions, mushrooms and carrots quickly. Add to casserole, cover tightly, and cook in a 300°F oven for 3 hours. Add peas last 20 minutes of cooking period. Adjust seasonings with salt and pepper. Garnish with chopped parsley.
Serves 4 to 6

Note: This dish may be prepared on top of the stove. Add onions and carrots the last 25 minutes of cooking time, the mushrooms and peas the last 10 minutes. Total cooking time is reduced to 2 hours. If additional liquid is needed, equal parts stock and wine may be added.

OXTAILS IN SOUR SAUCE WITH POTATO DUMPLINGS

3 pounds oxtails, disjointed
1 tablespoon vinegar
1 onion, chopped
1 bay leaf
1 teaspoon salt
1/2 teaspoon freshly ground pepper
1 tablespoon flour
1 tablespoon butter
4 tablespoons sour cream or yoghurt
potato dumplings (recipe follows)

Prepare oxtails according to Step I in basic instructions. Simmer in 1-1/2 pints water along with vinegar, onion, bay leaf, salt and pepper for 1-1/2 hours. Remove bay leaf. Blend together flour and butter, making a beurre manié (page 132). Stir into soup to thicken, continuing to cook 10 minutes longer. Stir in sour cream at the last minute; serve with potato dumplings.
Serves 4

POTATO DUMPLINGS

1 pound potatoes, boiled until
    tender in their skins
3 tablespoons or more flour
salt
1 egg
1 tablespoon cream

Peel and grate cooled potatoes. Mix with flour on a bread board; make a hollow in the center. Add salt, egg and cream and knead until smooth. Form into a large ball and pinch off small pieces, forming 1-inch balls. Cook in simmering, salted water for 20 minutes; drain. Serve with oxtails.

FILIPINO OXTAIL STEW

5 pounds oxtails, disjointed
5 tablespoons vegetable oil
1 large onion, thinly sliced
3 cloves garlic, finely chopped
5 pints beef stock or water
5 tablespoons rice or potato flour,
    toasted
6 to 8 tablespoons skinned peanuts,
    finely pulverized
1 pound fresh green beans
1 large aubergine, cut in wedges
sliced spring onions for garnish

Prepare oxtails according to basic instructions. Heat 3 tablespoons oil in flameproof casserole and brown tails on all sides. Remove and set aside; discard oil. Add remaining oil to casserole and sauté onion and garlic until transparent, about 6 to 8 minutes. Return oxtails and accumulated juices to casserole. Add stock, bring to a boil, reduce heat, cover and simmer for 2-1/2 hours, until meat is tender. Combine flour and peanuts and gradually stir into casserole. Add green beans and aubergine; turn and coat with liquids. Increase heat and cook, uncovered, for about 15 minutes, stirring occasionally. Garnish with onions. Serve piping hot with rice.
Serves 6

BRAISED OXTAILS, SPANISH STYLE

One of the greatest prizes bestowed upon a toreador after a brave fight in the bullring is the presentation of the bull's ears or tail. It is a culinary prize as well. In Seville, a restaurant may specialize in a dish called rabo de torro, made from the "sweet" tail meat of the bulls just killed in the ring. It is one of Andalusia's most renowned specialties.

2 oxtails, disjointed (about 3 to 4
  pounds)
3 tablespoons olive oil
2 onions, chopped
2 cloves garlic, finely chopped
1 tablespoon flour
1 pint beef stock
1/2 pint dry red wine
1/4 pint tomato sauce or thick fresh
  tomato purée
6 peppercorns
1/2 teaspoon crushed oregano
1 dried hot red chili, finely chopped
  and with seeds removed if desired
2 to 3 whole cloves
2 carrots, chopped
1 sweet red pepper, chopped
1 tablespoon chopped parsley
2 potatoes, cut into chunks (optional)
salt and freshly ground pepper to taste

Prepare oxtails according to Steps I and II in basic instructions; drain. Heat oil in a large, deep pan. Fry oxtails until browned. Remove from pan and set aside. Add onions and garlic to pan and brown. Add flour and cook 4 minutes; return oxtails to pan. Add stock, wine, tomato sauce, peppercorns, oregano, chili pepper and cloves. Stir to mix, cover and simmer 1-1/2 hours, or until meat is tender. Add carrots, red pepper, parsley and potatoes the last 30 minutes of cooking time.
Serves 6
Note: Meat and potatoes may be removed to a side dish and remaining sauce and vegetables pressed through a sieve. Return sauce to pan with meat and potatoes and heat through.

BRAISED OXTAILS WITH CHINESE CABBAGE

2-1/2 to 3 pounds oxtails, disjointed
2 tablespoons corn oil
1 clove garlic, finely chopped
1 slice fresh ginger root,
  finely chopped
2 tablespoons soy sauce
1 teaspoon salt
1/4 teaspoon Chinese 5-spice powder*
4 tablespoons dry sherry
generous 1/2 pint beef stock
1 teaspoon cornflour, mixed with
2 tablespoons water
1 head Chinese cabbage or Webb's
  lettuce, cut in wedges

Prepare oxtails according to Steps I and II in basic instructions. Heat oil with garlic and ginger; add oxtails to pan and brown. Add soy, salt, 5-spice powder, sherry and stock. Bring to a boil, reduce heat, cover and simmer 1-1/2 hours, or until meat is tender. Thicken juices with cornflour mixture. Simmer cabbage in another pot in salted water for 10 minutes, or until tender; drain. Pour oxtails over wedges.
Serves 6
*Available at Oriental stores

OTHER OFFAL

Giblets, spleen, lungs, fries, marrow and blood have all been used in a wide variety of cuisines. Yet, except for giblets, they generally go unnoticed.

Fries, marrow and blood are considered delicacies in many countries, especially in Europe. Spleen and lungs, though lacking the prominence and reverence accorded some of the other variety meats, are popular in some cuisines. Giblets, utilized more as a secondary ingredient than the others, are included because they probably are the most commonly used of all the innards.

Most dictionaries define giblets as any visceral organ of fowl. *Larousse Gastronomique* expands this definition to include the head, neck, pinions, feet, liver, cocks' comb and kidneys as well as the heart and gizzard of poultry. (It does exclude the liver of duck and geese, because in France they are given special treatment and are highly valued for their use in pâtés.) Thus it is not so surprising that the French word for giblets, *abatis*, has evolved as the general word for defining all offal or innards. We will define giblets to include only the heart and gizzard of any fowl.

Giblets are used for enhancing the flavor of stew or enriching stocks, if they are not cooked in a dish by themselves. A popular food among the Aztecs in Mexico, they were sold by vendors who specialized in prepared poultry giblets of ducks,

geese, waterfowl—practically all migratory birds. Along with the flesh and innards of the wild deer, the giblets of fowl were the most common meat in an otherwise mostly vegetarian society.

The spleen, also called melt (miltz by the Jewish populus), and lungs, or lights, most often have been used as ingredients in forcemeats and stuffings, as casings or in soups throughout the course of history. They have never reigned in splendor, but they were never thrown away either. In Renaissance Italy, the spleen, because of its sourness, was thought to be helpful to the stomach and the appetite, though it was thought one may quickly become full when eating it. The bulk of the recipes for spleen and lungs are found in the Central European, Jewish and Balkan cuisines. Stuffed miltz is a Jewish specialty; lungs are found in Viennese Kalbsbeuschel and and Turkish gömlek (chopped lambs' lungs baked with currants, dill and parsley).

Beef and lamb testicles are considered a great delicacy by the French, who call them *animelles*. In the United States, beef testicles are commonly called mountain or prairie oysters and lamb testicles are called fries. Fries have been eaten at banquets for centuries in Europe, and have been cooked over open fires by the Basques on the slopes of the Pyrenees. In the United States, the cowboys of the prairies enjoyed both fries and mountain oysters, especially when added to the famous son-of-a-bitch stew. The French, Spanish and Italians seem to be the only people who still recognize fries as a true delicacy.

Although rarely prepared by Americans, marrow is often served in European countries. Since the 14th century, it has been a popular first course on a French menu—fried, filled into miniature pastries or made into a pudding—and an important ingredient of sauces such as the *Marchand de Vin*.

It is interesting to note, however, that marrow played an important role in American history. Pemmican, a mixture of dried meat (jerky) pounded with fat, marrow and wild cherries, was prepared by the Cree indians of North America, and became a sustaining food of the explorers. It provided all that was necessary for warmth, energy and nourishment. Today, a lightweight version of pemmican is often carried by hikers.

Marrow was an important food of the cowboys of the early American West. Commonly called "prairie butter," they piled marrow atop their sourdough biscuits, an excellent substitute for butter. It was also an ingredient in Creole "Monday foods"—red beans and rice simmered with a cracked ham marrow bone.

Because the diet of the Eskimos consisted primarily of caribou (a very lean meat), they supplemented it with marrow. They boiled the bones in stews in order to obtain the necessary fat required to maintain body heat in the sub-zero temperatures of Northern Canada.

But the French have brought marrow its greatest fame. In one form or another—fried, baked, spread over or laid on top of tender meat, or stirred into sauces—marrow is an important ingredient in classic French cooking.

Blood played an important role in ancient rituals. In *Critias,* one of Plato's *Dialogues,* a description of the ancient island of Atlantis is given. Every four or five years the 10 kings who ruled the island met to discuss common affairs and the transgression of laws. They then slew one of the bulls that freely roamed in the sanctuary of Poseidon, mixed its blood with wine and drank the wine from golden beakers, vowing never to transgress from the laws again.

Blood was also one of the most characteristic foods of nomadic peoples. The Berber tribes of the ninth century drained blood from the veins of their cattle, mixed it with milk and drank it, while the Mongolian armies, carrying few provisions and traveling where food was scarce, tapped the veins of their steeds every 10 days or so and drank the blood uncooked. The Arabs, however, cooked the blood from their camels over an open fire before eating it.

Blood puddings were popular at medieval banquets and this popularity has carried over to the present day throughout Europe. Prepared blood (both in puddings and sausages) was one of the first items scrutinized for adulteration when meat inspection began in France in the 1300s. In Ireland in the 17th century, peasants bled their cows and boiled the blood with milk, butter and herbs. Drisheen, a blood pudding now famous in County Cork, is actually a version of this centuries-old dish. The bleeding of horses was also a common practice of early trappers and explorers in the days of the settlement of America. If the blood was not consumed in liquid form, it was preserved with salt, cut into squares and reserved for eating during times of scarcity.

The making of *boudin,* a sausage specialty of the country people of France, is rich in tradition. While the slaughtering of the pigs is done by the men of the family, the preparation of the *boudin* is left to the women. The making of *boudin* coincides with the pig killing, which most often is around Christmas, but may continue until Easter. We know of more than one occasion when grilled *boudin* has been enjoyed along with the first tomatoes.

A famous Filipino dish is *dinuguan* or "chocolate meat," pork and tripe cooked in blood. Some African tribes still drink fresh blood, or coagulate it and roast it over an open fire.

HUNTER'S GIBLET SOUP

giblets, wings and necks of
  2 wild ducks
1 onion, quartered
1 slice celeriac
1 clove garlic, crushed
1 teaspoon salt
8 tablespoons rice
1/4 teaspoon freshly grated nutmeg
salt and white pepper to taste
1 teaspoon lemon juice
1 tablespoon butter
1 tablespoon flour

Simmer duck parts with 1-1/2 pints water, onion, celeriac, garlic and salt for 1 hour, skimming away any scum that rises to the surface. Remove meat from bones and chop along with giblets. Strain stock. Add rice and simmer until soft. Then stir in chopped meat and giblets, seasonings and lemon juice. Blend butter and flour together, add in small bits to the soup and cook several minutes to thicken slightly.
Serves 4

GERMAN GIBLET SOUP

1 pound chicken, goose, turkey or
  duck giblets, including neck and
  feet and wings of small birds
3 tablespoons butter
1 onion, sliced
1 bay leaf
1 carrot, thinly sliced
1 turnip, thinly sliced
1 teaspoon salt
freshly ground pepper
1/2 pound tomatoes, peeled, seeded
  and chopped
3 tablespoons double cream

Quarter gizzards and halve livers (if not used for pâté!). Heat butter and sauté meats and onion for 5 minutes. Add 2-1/2 pints water, bay leaf, carrot, turnip, salt and pepper; simmer 45 minutes or longer. Remove necks, feet and wings, if used; discard. Add tomatoes and continue simmering for 5 minutes. Carefully stir in cream.
Serves 4

CHICKEN GIBLET SOUP WITH LEMON

3/4 pound chicken giblets
3 stalks celery with tops, sliced
3 cloves garlic, finely chopped
5 tablespoons or more lemon juice
1/2 pound courgettes, sliced
8 tablespoons rice
salt and freshly ground pepper

Clean and rinse giblets well. Place in soup pot with 3-1/2 pints water. Bring to a boil, skimming any scum that rises to surface; add celery, garlic and lemon juice and cover. Simmer for 1 hour. Remove giblets and chop; return to pot. Add courgettes and rice, and cook 15 minutes longer. Add the rice just before serving; heat through. Salt and pepper to taste.
Serves 6

Variation: One chicken carcass and its giblets may be substituted for the 3/4 pound giblets. Remove carcass before serving.

CHICKEN GIBLET GUMBO

1 pound chicken giblets, including
    necks
1/2 ham hock
1 bay leaf
1 clove garlic, finely chopped
2 tablespoons butter
1 onion, diced
2 stalks celery including tops, diced
2 green peppers, diced
1 pound tomatoes, peeled and diced
1 dried hot red chili, finely chopped
    (or more)
2 tablespoons chopped parsley
1/4 pound okra, sliced

Place giblets and necks in pot with ham hock, bay leaf, garlic and water to cover. Bring to a boil, reduce heat, cover and simmer for about 30 minutes. Remove giblets and chop coarsely; return to pot. Heat butter in frying pan; sauté onion, celery and peppers for 5 to 8 minutes. Then add to pot along with remaining ingredients; cook until okra is tender and stew is thickened. Remove necks, ham hock and bay leaf. Dice ham and return to pot. Serve with rice and a green salad.
Serves 6

WON TONS

1/2 pound lean minced pork
1/4 pound uncooked prawns, shelled
    and finely chopped
1/2 teaspoon fried sesame oil*
1 teaspoon soy sauce
1 teaspoon dry sherry
1 tablespoon cornflour
2 tablespoons finely chopped spring
    onions
1 egg
won ton skins* as needed,
    about 1 pound

Blend together all ingredients (mixture should be moist) and use for filling won ton skins. To fold won tons for soup: Place 1/2 teaspoon filling on lower right corner of won ton skin and roll to center, forming a triangle. Pinch close to filling, holding it in. Now pull the two acute angles down toward each other, keeping triangle flat. Pinch together at center, sealing with a drop of water. The ends remain free, resembling the tails or fins of a fish.
Bring 5 pints water to a boil and drop in the won tons. When they rise to the top, boil another minute or two. Drain, rinse with cool water and add to soup as directed in recipe.
*Available in Oriental stores

WAH WON TON

3-1/2 pints clarified chicken stock
1 slice fresh ginger root
8 dried Chinese mushrooms*, soaked to
    soften and sliced
6 chicken gizzards, sliced lengthwise
    1/8 inch thick
6 chicken hearts
6 chicken livers, halved
6 to 8 tablespoons sliced bamboo shoots
6 to 8 tablespoons sliced water
    chestnuts
1/4 pound mangetout peas
salt to taste
won tons (preceding)

Prepare won tons according to preceding recipe. Combine stock, mushrooms, ginger, gizzards and hearts in a pot; simmer for 30 minutes. Add livers, bamboo shoots and water chestnuts and simmer another 10 minutes. During last 5 minutes of cooking period, add mangetout peas and won tons; add salt to taste.
Serves 6
Note: Any combination of squid, shrimps, prawns, chicken or roast pork may be added to stock.
*Available in Oriental stores

RAGOUT OF CHICKEN GIBLETS

1 pound chicken giblets, halved
2 tablespoons vegetable oil or
    rendered chicken fat
1 onion, chopped
2 tablespoons chopped parsley
1 teaspoon cumin
3/4 pint chicken stock
2 potatoes, peeled and diced
4 tablespoons lemon juice
1 egg, beaten
2 tablespoons chopped fresh dill

Heat oil and sauté onion until transparent; add giblets and sauté until lightly browned. Add parsley, cumin and stock; cover and simmer for 30 minutes. Add potatoes and cook until soft. Stir in lemon juice. Pour 1/2 cup of cooking liquid slowly into egg, stirring constantly. Gradually add egg mixture to giblets. Stir in dill at last minute.
Serves 3 to 4

SAUTÉED GIZZARDS & HEARTS

1-1/2 pounds chicken gizzards
    and hearts
2 tablespoons flour
4 tablespoons butter or rendered
    chicken fat
1 teaspoon salt
1/4 teaspoon thyme
freshly ground pepper
4 tablespoons dry sherry or white wine
4 tablespoons chicken stock
1 clove garlic, finely chopped
1 green pepper, chopped
3 tablespoons chopped parsley
    for garnish

Clean giblets by trimming away any excess fat, dust with flour and brown in melted butter. Add remaining ingredients except green pepper and parsley. Cover and simmer 1 hour. Add the pepper during last 15 minutes of cooking time. Garnish with parsley and serve with rice or burghul (cracked) wheat.
Serves 4

Variation: For a Hungarian sauté, follow the above recipe, adding 1 teaspoon Hungarian paprika during cooking period. Then sauté 1/2 pound mushrooms in 2 tablespoons butter and add along with green pepper. Stir in 1/2 pint sour cream just before serving and heat through; do not boil. Serve on buttered noodles.

CHICKEN GIBLET RISOTTO

1 pound chicken giblets, diced
4 tablespoons butter or rendered
    chicken fat
6 to 8 tablespoons chopped spring
    onions
1 cup (about 6 ounces) long grain
    rice
3 cups hot chicken stock
pinch of saffron
1-1/2 teaspoons grated orange rind
salt and freshly ground pepper
1 small sweet red or green pepper,
    diced

Heat butter and sauté giblets, onions and rice for 10 to 15 minutes. Place in an oven proof casserole. Dissolve saffron in hot stock and pour into casserole along with orange rind and seasonings. Cover and place in a preheated 350°F oven for 45 minutes. During last 15 minutes of cooking period, add sweet peppers. Fluff with fork before serving.
Serves 4

STEAMED CHICKEN HEARTS & GIZZARDS

1 pound chicken hearts and gizzards
1 tablespoon soy sauce
1 tablespoon dry sherry
1 tablespoon peanut oil
1/2 teaspoon very finely chopped fresh
  ginger root
8 tablespoons diced ham
1 tablespoon very finely chopped
  choong toy* (preserved turnip)
6 to 8 tablespoons dried lily flowers*,
  soaked 10 minutes to soften and
  tied in knots
1 tablespoon cornflour

Slice gizzards lengthwise 1/8 inch thick. (If desired, hearts or gizzards may be used individually rather than combined.) Combine all ingredients in a shallow, ovenproof dish; spread mixture evenly over bottom of dish, making a slight indention in the middle. Place dish in a large steamer filled with water at least 2 inches deep. Cover with tight-fitting lid and steam for 45 minutes.

Serve with hot rice and a simple vegetable stir-fry, such as Chinese cabbage.
Serves 4
*Choong toy and dried lily flowers may be purchased at Oriental stores. Lily flowers are also known as golden needles and banana flowers.

CHINESE CHICKEN GIZZARDS

1 pound chicken gizzards, with fat
  (at least 3 tablespoons)
2 tablespoons soy sauce
2 tablespoons dry sherry
1 tablespoon sugar
1 slice fresh ginger root, very fineley
  chopped
1 piece dried tangerine peel*, soaked
  to soften and very finely chopped
1 cup chicken stock
2 whole star anise*
1 teaspoon salt
1 tablespoon cornflour, blended with
2 tablespoons cold water

Remove excessive fat from gizzards and reserve. Cut gizzards into 2 lobes (at center connective tissue). Then make crosswise slashes, 1/8 inch deep, on rounded side of each lobe.
Combine soy, sherry, sugar, ginger and tangerine peel and marinate gizzards for 1 hour. Render fat and heat to sizzling; add marinated gizzards, stir-frying until lightly browned, about 5 to 8 minutes. Add stock, star anise and salt. Bring to a boil, reduce heat, cover and simmer for 30 minutes. Thicken juices with cornflour mixture. Serve with hot rice or on toothpicks for an hors d'oeuvre.
Serves 4 as an entrée
*Available at Oriental stores

For a chicken gizzard stew: Follow the above recipe, adding sliced carrots, turnips, potatoes and celery to the gizzards after 20 minutes of cooking. Continue to cook until vegetables and gizzards are tender. Thicken juices with cornflour only if necessary.

GEFILTE MILTZ
(Stuffed Spleen)

1 ox spleen
2 tablespoons rendered chicken fat
1 onion, chopped
1 small green pepper, chopped
1 stalk celery, chopped
2 eggs
2 matzos, soaked in water for
    5 minutes and drained
2 tablespoons chopped parsley
1 teaspoon salt
1/2 teaspoon freshly ground pepper
1 pig's caul* (omit for kosher
    preparation)
3/4 pint beef stock

*Pig's caul is the fatty, net-like membrane investing the intestines, sometimes available on request from good butchers.

Remove outer membrane from spleen and make a lengthwise pocket. Scrape away 1/2 cup meat from inside of pocket; reserve. Heat fat and sauté onion, green pepper and celery for 2 minutes. Combine eggs with matzos and scraped meat from spleen in a mixing bowl. Add the sautéed vegetables, parsley and season, mixing well. (Mixture will resemble a thick batter.) Stuff this mixture into pocket; skewer or truss with white string. Wrap in a piece of caul fat. Place on rack of shallow roasting tin and pour stock over top. Bake in a 350°F oven for 1-1/2 hours, basting occasionally. Remove spleen and reduce cooking liquid, or thicken with cornflour blended with cold water. Serve sauce with baked spleen sliced in 1-inch-thick slices.
(For kosher preparation, rub prepared spleen with a tablespoon or more chicken fat or margarine before baking, rather than wrapping in caul fat.)
Serves 4 to 6

Variation on Stuffing

2 tablespoons butter
1 onion, chopped
2 stalks celery, chopped
1 large cooking apple, peeled, cored
    and sliced
8 tablespoons soft bread crumbs or
    diced raw potatoes
5 tablespoons raisins, soaked in
    cider to soften
1 egg
1 teaspoon salt
1/2 teaspoon freshly ground pepper
3/4 pint cider for cooking liquid

Follow the preceding recipe for preparation of spleen. Sauté vegetables and combine with remaining substituted ingredients. Wrap in caul fat and pour cider over spleen. Continue as in preceding recipe.

PREPARATION OF FRIES

The culinary term for the testicles of male animals is fries (mountain or prairie oysters in the United States) or *animelles* in France. Generally speaking, the testicles of beef are called mountain or prairie oysters and the testicles of lamb are called fries, though the term fries is sometimes used to refer to both beef and lamb.

Step I: Cleaning and Rinsing
To clean fries, remove the outer skin or sac by slicing through sac near the testicle (or head). Push testicle through slit in sac. Separate sac from testicles by cutting the connecting duct away from testicle. Discard sac. Rinse in cold running water until water runs clear. Drain well.

Step II: Parboiling
Parboil in salted water (1 tablespoon salt for each 1-1/2 pints water) 5 minutes for lamb, 15 minutes for beef. Drain well before using.

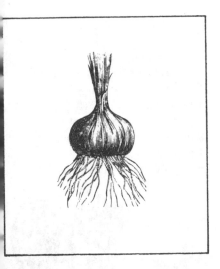

SAUTÉED FRIES

Fries from small animals, such as veal or lamb, should be cleaned first, then rolled in flour and dipped into beaten egg. Roll another time in fine French bread crumbs and then sauté in butter until brown.

Fries from large animals, such as beef, should be cleaned and split in half lengthwise. Then marinate fries in an herb-flavored vinaigrette for an hour or so. Roll in a mixture of flour and cornmeal and fry in hot deep fat until golden brown. Salt and pepper to taste. Serve with lemon wedges.

BRAISED MOUNTAIN OYSTERS AND BROCCOLI

1/2 pound mountain oysters (page 124)
1 clove garlic, finely chopped
1 slice fresh ginger root, finely chopped
1 tablespoon soy sauce
2 tablespoons dry sherry
1 tablespoon sugar
2 slices bacon, diced
1 onion, sliced
1-1/2 pounds broccoli, broken into flowerets and stems trimmed and sliced 1/4 inch thick
1 tablespoon cornflour, blended with
4 tablespoons water

Prepare mountain oysters according to Steps I and II in basic instructions. Slice in half lengthwise, then in 1/8-inch slices. Marinate the slices with the garlic, ginger, soy, sherry, and sugar for 30 minutes. Stir-fry the bacon in its own fat, add onions and marinated meat until meat is well seared and brown. Add 1/4 pint water, cover and cook over medium heat for 15 minutes; then add broccoli and cover again until steam rises to top, keeping broccoli tender-crisp. Thicken juices with the cornflour mixture. Serve with hot rice.
Serves 4

LAMB FRIES CLEROU

2 pounds lamb fries
2 tablespoons butter
3 strips bacon, diced
1 onion, chopped
3 or more cloves garlic, finely chopped
8 tablespoons chopped parsley
1/4 pint tomato sauce or thick fresh tomato purée
1/4 pint dry white wine
1/4 pint beef stock
1/2 teaspoon summer savory or rosemary
salt and freshly ground pepper to taste
1 or more dried hot red chilis, finely chopped
2 tablespoons Madeira or brandy

Prepare lamb fries according to Steps I and II in basic instructions. Melt butter and render bacon in a wide, deep pan. Sauté onion, garlic and parsley for 5 minutes. Add fries and brown. Combine tomato sauce, wine and stock and pour in barely enough liquid to cover the fries. Add seasonings. Simmer over low heat for 45 minutes, adding more liquid as necessary. At end of cooking period deglaze the pan with Madeira or brandy. Serve with crusty French bread and a green salad.
Serves 6

PREPARATION OF MARROW

Marrow is savored for its rich and creamy flavor and is served closer to its natural form than any other offal. The best marrow comes from leg bones and is often used as a flavor enrichment for soups, stews and sauces. But nothing could be better than spreading marrow on French bread and toasting it under the grill. When the marrow has melted (the fat content is high), remove and sprinkle with coarsely ground pepper, salt and lemon juice. Serve piping hot.

If you prefer, the marrow bones (about 1-1/2 to 2 inches long) may be baked in the oven at 350°F for 25 to 30 minutes and served along with toast or French bread. Each person then removes marrow from bones.

SUGGESTIONS FOR SERVING MARROW

• Rub marrow into lean meats for added flavor and to keep them from drying out. For instance, sliced liver steaks, heart or kidneys may be rubbed with marrow, coarsely ground pepper and garlic before grilling.
• Serve baked marrow bones for a first course with thin toast.
• When grilling a steak, place a slice of marrow on it after it is turned.

MARROW DUMPLINGS

4 tablespoons fresh marrow (scraped from bone cavity of leg bones preferably)
2 tablespoons butter
2 eggs, beaten
1/2 teaspoon salt
dash of freshly ground pepper
1/4 teaspoon freshly grated nutmeg
2 tablespoons finely chopped parsley
approximately 4 ounces fine dry bread or cracker crumbs
1/2 teaspoon baking powder
stock as needed

Combine all ingredients, except stock, and beat until smooth, adding enough bread crumbs for mixture to hold its shape. Shape into 1/2-inch balls. Cook in boiling stock for 10 to 15 minutes. Remove with slotted spoon. Serve with plain stock or with stewed chicken and vegetables.
Serves 4

MARROW & APPLE PIE

8 tablespoons raisins
8 tablespoons Calvados, rum or Port
5 pounds marrow bones
1 teaspoon salt
2 pounds tart baking apples
8 tablespoons sugar
1 tablespoon cornflour
pastry for 10-inch pie (page 134)

APPLE PARER.

Soak raisins in Calvados. Put marrow bones on a baking sheet and place in a 350°F oven for 15 minutes. Scoop marrow from bones when cool enough to handle, slice and sprinkle with salt.
Peel and slice apples. Line pie dish with pastry. Add apples, sugar, cornflour, marrow and raisins with Calvados; cover with top crust. Bake for 15 minutes in a preheated 425°F oven; reduce heat to 350°F and bake for about 45 minutes, or until crust is golden and filling is cooked through.

SANGUETTE

This is a popular dish in the country where people kill their own chickens and rabbits. In France, you'll even find sanguette available in provincial restaurants. It's a specialty of Orne, in the province of Normandy.

A chicken or rabbit is bled into a dish containing garlic and parsley, even a strip of bacon on occasion. Then the fresh blood is quickly fried in goose fat or lard. Remove to a heated shallow platter and deglaze pan with 1 tablespoon or more cider vinegar. Pour over fried blood and serve with French bread or toast rounds.

DRISHEEN

This is a traditional black or blood pudding from County Cork. Originally, drisheen was made from fresh sheep's blood but pig's blood may be substituted.

1-1/2 pints fresh sheep's or pig's blood
3/4 pint cream or creamy milk, scalded and cooled
8 tablespoons oatmeal
1/2 teaspoon freshly ground pepper
1 teaspoon salt
1/8 teaspoon mace
1 sprig thyme
pork casings (page 79)

Combine all ingredients and stuff into pork casings as per boudin (see page 87). If preferred, mixture may be poured into ramekins or earthenware bowl and baked in a pan of hot water for 1 hour at 300°F. Serve warm or cold. This is delicious sliced and fried or grilled for breakfast or supper accompanied by scrambled eggs and rashers of bacon.
Makes about 3 pounds sausages

HUNTERS' BLOOD PUDDING

Any freshly killed bird—a goose, chicken or duck—may be used for this recipe.

about 1/2 pint fresh blood
4 tablespoons rendered poultry fat
3 onions, finely chopped
4 tablespoons finely chopped parsley
1 green pepper, finely chopped
2 cloves garlic, finely chopped
salt and freshly ground pepper

Heat fat and sauté onions, parsley, pepper and garlic. Quickly add blood, sauté, stirring constantly, for 5 minutes. Season to taste with salt and pepper. Serve hot on buttered pumpernickel or black bread with mustard and pickles for a first course; add grilled tomatoes, cheese and fruit for a light supper.
Serves 4 to 6

MIXED MEAT FONDUE

This is a different version of the familiar beef fondue. Select several innards—cubes of calf liver, whole chicken livers, quartered lamb or cubes of veal kidneys, parboiled slices of sweetbreads and brains—and arrange on a platter; garnish with watercress. Combine equal amounts unsalted butter and cooking oil in a fondue pot and heat to sizzling. Place the fondue pot over an alcohol burner on the table along with the platter of meats and fresh vegetables such as whole mushrooms and chunks of green pepper. Each guest makes his own selections and sizzles them to his liking. Have a selection of sauces and/or condiments for dipping—Béarnaise sauce, horseradish blended into whipped cream, Dijon-style mustard, dill-flavored sour cream, chutney, sea salt and freshly crushed or coarsely ground black pepper. Then, of course, lots of crusty French bread and red wine.

EASTER LAMB
(Stuffed Suckling Lamb)

The traditional Easter meat in Greece is a spit-roasted suckling lamb, filled with a rice stuffing to which almost all the innards—heart, liver, sweetbreads, etc.—are added.

1 8- to 10-pound suckling lamb,
    cleaned, with head, neck and
    feet removed
salt
juice of 1/2 lemon
4 tablespoons butter
1 lamb heart, chopped
2 lamb kidneys, chopped
1 onion, chopped
1/2 cup (about 3 ounces) rice
2 tablespoons chopped fresh mint
2 tablespoons chopped parsley
1/8 teaspoon cinnamon
1/4 teaspoon freshly ground pepper
1 cup chicken stock
3 ounces raisins, plumped in dry
    white wine
1/2 pint tomato juice
branches of fresh oregano or rosemary

Wash lamb inside and out; pat dry. Rub inside cavity with salt; then rub salt and lemon juice into outside flesh. Heat butter in large saucepan and sauté heart and kidneys until lightly browned. Add onion and cook until transparent. Then add rice, herbs, spices and stock. Simmer, uncovered, until most of liquid is absorbed. Then cover and cook for 20 minutes. Stir in raisins. Stuff this mixture into cavity of lamb and truss with white string or skewer together securely.

Cook on a turning spit. Tie branches of oregano together and use for basting brush; baste with tomato juice once meat starts to brown. Barbecue over glowing charcoal for 1-1/2 to 2 hours. Or, if your oven will take it, place in a roasting tin in a 300°F oven, allowing about 40 minutes per pound. Baste with tomato juice once meat starts to brown. Serve with a Greek salad, bread and wine. A sumptuous feast.

Serves 6 to 8

MIXED LAMB KEBAB

1 pound lamb liver
1 pound lamb heart
1 pound lamb kidneys (prepare
   according to Steps I and II,
   Kidneys)
6 to 8 tablespoons very finely chopped
   onions
2 cloves garlic, finely chopped
6 to 8 tablespoons lemon juice
4 tablespoons olive oil
1/2 teaspoon coarsely ground pepper
4 slices bacon, cut in 1-inch pieces
1 small aubergine, unpeeled and
   cut in 1-inch chunks
1/2 pound courgettes, cut in
   1-inch chunks
flour
light batter (see fritto misto,
   page 131)
oil for deep-frying

Remove arteries and veins from hearts. Cut all meats in 1-inch chunks. Combine onions, garlic, lemon juice, olive oil and ground pepper and marinate meats for 2 hours. Drain, then skewer alternately with bacon, aubergine and courgettes.

Dust lightly with flour and dip in the prepared batter. Fry in hot, deep fat until crisp and golden. Serve with fresh tomatoes, dressed in a sweet basil or coriander-flavored vinaigrette.

Serves 8 to 10

Variation: To barbecue kebabs follow the above recipe, omitting batter. Blanch courgettes for 1 minute or cut in 1/2-inch chunks before threading on skewers. Cook over hot charcoal, basting frequently with remaining marinade, for 5 to 7 minutes on each side.

MIXED MEAT KEBABS

Heart, kidneys and liver—of any variety and in any combination—make particularly good kebabs. Cut meats into 1- to 1-1/2-inch cubes (leave chicken innards whole) and thread on metal or bamboo skewers. Marinate for at least 3 hours to adequately tenderize and flavor meat. Grill over hot charcoal, basting often and turning and being especially careful not to overcook.

You may also alternate the meats with mushroom slices, green pepper chunks, tiny red tomatoes, bacon strips (for extra moisture), Spanish onion chunks, button onions (parboiled 5 minutes), sweet pepper chunks or whatever else sounds good.

Each of the following marinades is sufficient for 3 pounds of meat. Combine all ingredients listed and marinate meats for at least 3 hours, or overnight in the refrigerator.

HERB MARINADE

1/2 pint olive oil
1/4 pint red wine
2 onions, chopped
2 sprigs thyme
2 bay leaves
1 teaspoon freshly ground pepper
1/2 teaspoon salt
3 cloves garlic, finely chopped

TURKISH MARINADE

1/4 pint olive oil
1/4 pint lemon juice
1/2 teaspoon cinnamon
salt and coarsely ground pepper

CHINESE MARINADE

4 tablespoons soy sauce
4 tablespoons dry sherry
2 tablespoons corn oil
1/2 teaspoon fried sesame oil*
2 cloves garlic, finely chopped
1 teaspoon finely chopped fresh
    ginger root
1 teaspoon sugar
1 tablespoon chopped fresh
    coriander (optional)
1 tablespoon chopped spring onions

Variation: Omit soy sauce; add 4 tablespoons Chinese hoisin sauce and 1/2
teaspoon 5-spice powder, both available
in Oriental stores.
*The dark seasoning oil available in
Oriental stores.

GREEK MARINADE

6 to 8 tablespoons olive oil
5 tablespoons lemon juice
2 onions, very finely chopped
2 bay leaves, crushed
1 teaspoon crushed oregano
1/4 pint sieved tomato pulp
salt and coarsely ground pepper

YOGHURT MARINADE

1/2 pint plain yoghurt
8 tablespoons chopped fresh mint
1 onion, very finely chopped
2 cloves garlic, finely chopped
salt and coarsely ground pepper

MIXED GRILL

6 rib lamb chops
6 small slices calf liver, brushed
    with butter
12 large mushroom caps, brushed
    with butter
6 slices bacon
6 lamb kidneys, split
6 tomatoes, halved
potato straws
watercress for garnish

Grill lamb chops, liver and mushrooms 4 to 5 minutes on each side. Grill bacon until crisp. Then grill kidneys and tomatoes a total of 5 minutes. Arrange potatoes in the middle of a large, heated platter; surround with meats and tomatoes. Garnish with watercress.
Serves 6

FRITTO MISTO

This famous Italian mixed fry is made up of an assortment of offal meats—chicken and calf liver, kidneys, brains, sweetbreads—and may include chunks of chicken breast or veal as well. Like the Japanese tempura, vegetables are very much a part of the dish. Artichoke hearts, slices of courgette and aubergine, mushrooms and/or cauliflowerets are served along with the meats. Cut all the selected foods in equal-sized pieces. The sweetbreads, brains and vegetables should be parboiled. All of the ingredients are then dipped into a rich batter and fried in deep, hot fat (380°F on a frying thermometer) until golden. Generally speaking, the fat is a combination of olive oil and unsalted butter (about 2-1/2 pints olive oil to 1/4 pound butter). It is essential to maintain a hot temperature; reduced temperatures and crowding cause sogginess. As foods are fried, remove to a warm platter and serve immediately. When all the ingredients have been fried, sprinkle with salt and serve with lemon wedges.

BATTER

1 tablespoon melted butter
2 eggs, well beaten
1/4 pint milk or cream
1/4 pound plain flour, sifted
1/2 teaspoon salt
1/4 teaspoon white pepper

Combine all ingredients and beat until smooth. Let batter stand about 20 minutes before using. Dry all meats well before dipping them into batter.

BASICS

BEURRE MANIÉ

To make a beurre manié, use your fingers to combine equal parts flour and butter, making a crumbly mixture. Sprinkle the grains gradually into hot liquid. Use for thickening soups and sauces.

BOUQUET GARNI

2 to 4 sprigs parsley
1/4 teaspoon thyme
1 small bay leaf

Wrap herbs together in a piece of washed cheesecloth and tie securely. Use for flavoring stocks, soups, stews, sauces and braised meats.
Note: Additional herbs may be added to the bouquet garni, if desired, including chervil, tarragon, rosemary, basil, etc.

PICKLING OR CORNING BRINE

To each gallon of cold water add:
1-1/2 cups rock salt or sea salt
1 cup dark brown sugar
2 to 3 tablespoons saltpetre*
any combination of spices such as
    whole peppercorns, allspice, cloves,
    bay leaves, garlic cloves, fresh
    ginger slices, crushed juniper
    berries, mustard seeds and
    blades of mace

Boil all ingredients for 5 minutes. Allow to cool and strain before pouring over meat.
Note: One of our favorite combinations of spices is 2 bay leaves, 8 peppercorns and 4 crushed juniper berries.
*Saltpetre (sodium nitrate) is available from many chemists. It is responsible for the pink color taken on by the meat.

VINAIGRETTE DRESSING

generous 1/4 pint olive oil
5 tablespoons wine vinegar
1 tablespoon lemon juice
1 teaspoon salt
freshly ground pepper to taste
1 teaspoon finely chopped chives
1 tablespoon finely chopped parsley
1/2 teaspoon tarragon

Combine all ingredients and mix or beat well to form an emulsion.

Variation: Follow the above recipe, omitting tarragon. Substitute 1 or 2 cloves garlic, finely chopped. Just before serving, stir in 4 tablespoons more finely chopped parsley and 2 spring onions with tops, finely chopped. This is the same vinaigrette the Basques use for their white beans. The additional parsley and spring onions are stirred into the already marinated beans just before serving.

BÉCHAMEL SAUCE

2 tablespoons butter
4 tablespoons finely chopped onion
4 tablespoons flour
scant 1/2 pint court bouillon or stock
scant 1/2 pint milk

Melt the butter in a pan, add onions and cook for 2 minutes. Then add flour, blend well and cook another 2 minutes. Gradually add the stock and milk and cook until thickened.
Makes about 3/4 pint

SAUCE GRIBICHE

1 tablespoon Dijon-style mustard or
   to taste
1 tablespoon wine vinegar
generous 1/4 pint olive oil
salt and freshly ground pepper to taste
1 tablespoon chopped fresh herbs
   (parsley, chervil or chives or
   in combination), or
1 teaspoon chopped fresh thyme
1 tablespoon chopped gherkins
2 teaspoons chopped capers
1 hard-boiled egg, yolk finely
   sieved and white cut into julienne
   strips

Combine all ingredients and mix well. Allow several hours for flavors to blend. Excellent as a garnish for head-cheese, cold cuts, pâtés and terrines.
Makes about 1/2 pint

BÉARNAISE SAUCE

8 tablespoons white wine vinegar
1 tablespoon finely chopped shallots or
   whites of spring onion
1 tablespoon fresh chopped tarragon, or
1 teaspoon dried tarragon leaves
pinch of salt and freshly ground pepper
3 egg yolks
4 tablespoons softened butter

Combine the vinegar, shallots, tarragon, salt and pepper and cook over medium heat until reduced to 2 tablespoons. Do not burn. Cool. In the top of a double boiler, over hot (not boiling) water, beat the egg yolks with the vinegar mixture, using a wire whisk, until thick. Add a tablespoon of butter at a time, beating until melted; repeat, until all butter has been added. Serve this sauce lukewarm.
Makes a generous 1/2 pint
Note: If this sauce should accidentally curdle (water too hot), let it cool to lukewarm, then whirl in a blender for a couple of seconds.

HOT TOMATO SAUCE

1 onion, finely chopped
2 tablespoons olive oil
1-1/2 pounds ripe tomatoes, peeled,
   seeded and chopped
3 tablespoons lemon juice
salt and freshly ground pepper to taste
1 teaspoon grated lemon rind

Sauté onions in olive oil. Add chopped tomatoes and lemon juice; bring to a boil and simmer 5 minutes. Season to taste with salt and pepper. Add the lemon rind and more juice to taste just before serving.
Makes approximately 1-1/2 pints

COLD TOMATO SAUCE

1 pound ripe tomatoes, peeled and
   chopped
2 hot green (fresh) chilis, peeled
   and chopped*
2 tablespoons olive oil
2 tablespoons red wine vinegar
1/2 onion, finely chopped
1 clove garlic, finely chopped
1/2 teaspoon crushed oregano
1 tablespoon chopped fresh coriander
salt and freshly ground pepper to taste

Combine all ingredients, allowing 2 to 3 hours for flavors to blend.
Makes about 3/4 pint

*Remove seeds if a milder flavor is preferred. Or substitute 2 to 3 teaspoons paprika to taste.

RICH SHORTCRUST PASTRY

8 ounces unbleached white flour, sifted
1 teaspoon salt
6 ounces white vegetable fat (or part
   butter)
about 4 tablespoons cold water

Combine the flour and salt in a mixing bowl. Cut in the fat with a pastry blender. Sprinkle the water, a table-spoon at a time, mixing well with a fork until all the flour is moistened. With hands, gather the dough into a ball. Divide in two and roll each ball of dough to 1/8 inch thickness. May be frozen for later use. Makes enough pastry for a 2-crust 9- or 10-inch pie or tart.

PUFF PASTRY

8 ounces plain flour
1/2 teaspoon salt
about 5 tablespoons ice water
8 ounces unsalted butter, very cold

Sift the flour and salt on a board. Make a well in center. Stir in water with fingers; knead dough until smooth and elastic. Roll dough into a rectangle about 1/4 inch thick. Cut the butter in thirds, lengthwise. Place the butter slices in the center of the dough, the length of the rectangle. Fold one flap over the butter and bring the other flap on top. This makes 3 layers and should cover the butter entirely. Press the side edges together to prevent butter from "ooz-ing" out. Chill the dough for 30 min-utes. Place the chilled dough on board and roll into a longer rectangle. Dough should be rolled as thin as possible without the butter coming through. If butter breaks through, it means air is being lost (enclosed air puffs the paste). Fold the rectangle again in thirds, this time "pressed" edges over center, and other edge over top. This is called a "turn." Chill again for 30 min-utes. Repeat 4 more times, chilling and rolling after every turn. Dough may be chilled or frozen at this point. Be sure to wrap well with plastic wrap, to pre-vent drying out in refrigerator or freezer. Use as needed.

CORNMEAL TORTILLAS

6 ounces strong white flour
6 ounces yellow cornmeal
4 tablespoons corn oil
3/4 teaspoon salt
generous 1/4 pint lukewarm water
corn oil as needed for frying

Mix together the flour, cornmeal, oil and salt by hand. Gradually add enough water to make a firm but pliable dough, mixing well with your hands. Turn out the dough on to a floured board and knead vigorously for at least 3 minutes. Separate dough into 12 pieces and with your hands, roll each piece into a ball. Let stand 15 minutes. On a floured board roll each ball of dough into a pancake about 6 inches in diameter. Fry the tortillas on a lightly greased griddle or heavy frying pan, turning them 2 or 3 times, until cooked but not browned. Stack and leave to cool. Store the tortillas sealed in plastic wrap in the refrigerator or freezer.
Makes 1 dozen tortillas

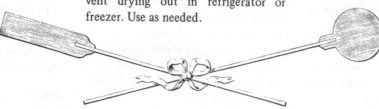

REFRIED BEANS
(Frijoles Refritos)

3/4 pound red kidney beans
1/2 teaspoon oregano
salt to taste
1/4 pound lard
1/4 pound mild Cheddar cheese,
  coarsely grated

Wash and soak beans overnight in 3-1/2 pints cold water. Add salt and oregano and simmer in same liquid, covered, until beans are tender, about 1-1/2 hours. (Beans should be well cooked.) Drain, reserving liquid; mash beans well. Melt lard in a heavy frying pan and bring almost to smoking point. Carefully add mashed beans and cook over low heat, stirring frequently, until lard is absorbed. More lard may be added if desired. Beans may also be thinned out to desired consistency with some of the reserved cooking liquid. Add cheese, mix well and cook until completely melted. Continue to cook 15 minutes.
Serves 6 to 8
Note: If you prefer spicier beans, sauté onions, garlic and/or dried hot red chilis in the lard until onions are transparent before adding the beans.

MEXICAN RICE

2 cups (about 3/4 pound) long grain
  rice, washed and well drained
3 to 4 tablespoons lard
1 medium-size onion, chopped
1 or more cloves garlic, finely chopped
1/2 teaspoon cumin
4 tablespoons tomato sauce or thick
  fresh tomato purée
salt to taste

Sauté rice in melted lard until lightly browned. Add chopped onion, garlic and cumin and continue cooking until onions are limp. Add tomato sauce and salt. Add 3-1/2 cups water to rice. Bring to a rapid boil, lower heat to medium and continue cooking, uncovered, until all the liquid has been absorbed. Then lower heat to simmer, cover and continue cooking for 15 minutes.
Serves 8

SWEET VEGETABLE RELISH

This is a crisp, refreshing relish that is good served with almost any meat, but especially barbecued meats such as kebabs.

1 pound carrots, scraped and sliced on
  diagonal 1/8 inch thick
1 large green pepper, cut in
  1-inch chunks
1 sweet red pepper, cut in 1-inch
  chunks
2 onions, cut in 1-inch chunks
1 cucumber, unpeeled, seeded and
  cut in 1-inch chunks
6 to 8 tablespoons thinly sliced fresh
  ginger root
1 or more dried hot red chilis
1/2 pint wine vinegar
7 ounces sugar
1/2 teaspoon salt

Prepare all vegetables. Then combine ginger root, dried chilis, vinegar, sugar and salt with 1/4 pint water in a saucepan. Bring to a rapid boil, reduce heat and simmer for 5 minutes; remove from heat, cool to tepid and add carrots. Cool completely, stirring from time to time. Add green pepper, sweet red pepper, onions and cucumber. Pour into a bowl and chill at least 4 hours, or overnight, in the refrigerator. May be stored in the refrigerator up to 3 days.
Makes approximately 2-1/2 pints

WEIGHTS & MEASURES

The recipes in this book were originally devised and tested using American cup and spoon measures. These have been converted to fractions of pounds, ounces and pints where it seemed most practical. However, in some cases, where comparative volumes are more important to the success of a dish, the original cup measures have been retained.

The American cup holds 8 fluid ounces, the equivalent of a medium-sized teacup, and 2 cups, or 16 fluid ounces, make 1 American pint. (The Imperial pint holds 20 fluid ounces, or one-fifth more, and whenever pints have been used it is the 20-ounce pint that is meant.) However, provided the same cup is used throughout a recipe, a slight discrepancy will not matter. What is important is that cups, tablespoons and teaspoons should always be measured level.

For those who wish to use metric measures, the equivalents, adjusted to the nearest con-venient figure, are as follows (volume and weight).

Should you wish to make a more accurate conversion (particularly useful for baking, etc.), the exact equivalents are:

1 ounce	=	28.35	grammes
16 ounces	=	453.6	grammes
1 pint	=	568	millilitres
1 kilo	=	2.2	pounds
1 litre	=	1.76	pints
1 decilitre	=	100	millilitres

OUNCES/FLUID OUNCES		GRAMMES/MILLILITRES
½	=	15
1	=	25
2	=	50
3	=	75
4 (¼ pound)	=	100–110
5 (¼ pint)	=	150 (1½ decilitres)
6	=	175
7	=	200 (2 decilitres)
8 (½ pound)	=	225 (use ¼ kilo)
9	=	250 (2½ decilitres = ¼ kilo)
10 (½ pint)	=	275 (use 2½ decilitres)
11	=	300 (3 decilitres)
12	=	350 (3½ decilitres)
13	=	375
14	=	400 (4 decilitres)
15 (¾ pint)	=	425 (4½ decilitres)
16 (1 pound)	=	450 (4½ decilitres)
17	=	475
18	=	500 (5 decilitres = ½ kilo)
19	=	550 (5½ decilitres)
20 (1 pint)	=	575 (use 5½ decilitres)

The oven temperatures in this book are given in °F. Gas Regulo and Celsius (Centigrade) equivalents are as follows:

	FAHRENHEIT		GAS MARK		CELSIUS
very cool	225	=	¼	=	110
very cool	250	=	½	=	130
cool	275	=	1	=	140
very slow	300	=	2	=	150
slow	325	=	3	=	160
moderate	350	=	4	=	180
moderate	375	=	5	=	190
moderately hot	400	=	6	=	200
fairly hot	425	=	7	=	220
hot	450	=	8	=	230
very hot	475	=	9	=	240
extremely hot	500	=	10	=	250

INDEX

ABOUT THE AUTHORS

The collaboration of Jana Vaughan Allen and Margaret Lee Gin brings together the culinary heritages of Europe and the Far East in the preparation of offal and other variety meats.

Jana Allen, at present assistant food editor of the *San Francisco Chronicle,* was raised in Bakersfield, California, near the large Basque shepherding community in the foothills of the lower San Joaquin Valley. As a child here she developed an early interest in food and a taste for offal, attending many French-Basque gatherings in which food played a major role. Since graduating from Oregon State University, Jana Allen has traveled extensively in Mexico and Europe, always sampling and studying the cuisines of the countries visited. Before joining the *Chronicle* food staff, she taught a course in Regional and Foreign Foods at San Marin High School in Marin County. Her articles have been published in *Bon Appétit* and other periodicals.

Margaret Gin's culinary background is a unique combination of Chinese and the American West. Her parents were raised in Canton and settled in Tucson, where they owned a grocery store featuring homemade American pastry. As a young girl she mastered the preparation of Chinese stir-fry cooking, while learning to prepare spicy Mexican dishes with equal ease. After moving to San Francisco, her Oriental banquets became so renowned that at friends' urging, she began teaching Chinese cooking classes. Mrs. Gin is the author of several cookery books, including *Regional Cooking of China* (due for UK publication in 1977).